CHRIST AND THE DESERT TABERNACLE

CHRIST AND THE DESERT TABERNACLE

J. V. FESKO

EP BOOKS
Faverdale North, Darlington, DL3 0PH, England

e-mail: sales@epbooks.org
web: http://www.epbooks.org

© John V. Fesko 2012

All rights reserved. No part of this publication may be reproduced, stored in a retrieval system or transmitted, in any form, or by any means, electronic, mechanical, photocopying, recording or otherwise, without the prior permission of the publishers.

First published 2012

British Library Cataloguing in Publication Data available

ISBN-13: 978-0-85234-781-2   ISBN-10: 0-85234-781-2

Unless otherwise indicated, all Scripture quotations are from The Holy Bible, English Standard Version, published by HarperCollins Publishers © 2001 by Crossway Bibles, a division of Good News Publishers. Used by permission. All rights reserved.

Printed and bound in Great Britain by the MPG Books Group, Bodmin and King's Lynn.

*Dedicated to the
tireless service of elders*

Wallace B. King

and

Carleton 'Bud' Winslow

ACKNOWLEDGEMENTS

I want to express my thanks to David Woollin for his interest in pursuing the idea of publishing this book. I am also very thankful for the staff at EP for their diligent effort in reading early drafts of the manuscript, offering helpful suggestions, and seeing this book to press.

I am also thankful to my wife, for her constant support, love and encouragement. As the old song goes, 'You've got a smile so bright, you could've been a candle!' I am grateful to our faithful covenant Lord that he has given her and our boys, Val and Rob, to me.

In many ways this book is about the ultimate church-building programme. Though it begins with the blueprints for the tabernacle, these portions of Scripture are ultimately about Christ, the cornerstone, and the final dwelling place made out of living stones, the church. As I have reflected upon these texts, my mind has been drawn back repeatedly to my time in the pastorate at Geneva Orthodox Presbyterian Church (Woodstock, Georgia), where this book originated as part of a sermon series on Exodus. I have been reminded not merely of the Sundays when I delivered the messages but of my own small efforts to build, care for and protect the small section of God's final dwelling place that Geneva represents. I did not work alone. The love, care, labours, prayers and ceaseless shepherding of my two ruling elders, Wallace B. King and Carleton 'Bud' Winslow, were indispensible. These two men gave up countless hours on behalf of the saints at Geneva. They continue to labour in this way to the present. Bud and Wally, thank you for your tireless service to Christ's church. It is to you, dear brothers, that I dedicate this book. May our faithful triune Lord continue to bless your labours as you build the final dwelling place of our triune Lord.

J. V. Fesko
Escondido, California
September 2012

CONTENTS

		Page
Introduction		11
1.	Building materials	13
2.	The Ark of the Covenant	21
3.	The table and the bread of presence	29
4.	The lampstand and oil	39
5.	The tabernacle	49
6.	The altar and courtyard	57
7.	The priest's garments	67
8.	The consecration of the priests	77
9.	The altar of incense	85
10.	The census tax	95
11.	The bronze basin	105
12.	Oholiab and Bezalel	115
13.	The Sabbath	125
Conclusion		133

INTRODUCTION

I can remember sitting at the breakfast table, bleary-eyed, at six o'clock in the morning reading my Bible for family devotions. My parents had decided that we would read through the Bible in a year. Like most people in the church I found the opening chapters of the Old Testament to be interesting — the narratives had many fascinating and exciting accounts of the lives of the saints. Some of the narratives that come to mind are the sacrifice of Isaac (Gen. 22) and the Red Sea crossing (Exod. 14). But soon after the Israelites emerged from the Red Sea and received the Ten Commandments (Exod. 20), to my young and perhaps sleepy mind, the narrative came to a screeching halt when we began reading about the tabernacle. I can remember reading about the various pieces of furniture, the curtains, the priest's clothing, and thinking that there were too many details, and frankly, they were boring. To a child's mind, how can Pharaoh's army drowning in the Red Sea compare to a table with bread, or a washbasin? In one sense, my lack of interest of the Bible was understandable — I was a young child who did not know better. On the other hand, as a pastor I also know of people with whom I have discussed passages about the tabernacle who have told me that they find them uninteresting and often skip over them during their devotional reading.

In the pages that follow, I hope to be able to show readers, young and old alike, that far from being boring or uninteresting, the Old Testament tabernacle, and later the temple in Solomon's day, is a shadowy picture of Christ and the church. True, people are perhaps easily able to draw the connections between Jesus and the sacrificial animals, as Jesus is identified as the one and only true sacrifice who takes away our sins (e.g., Heb. 8-10; 1 John 2:2); but beyond these obvious connections, the Old Testament tabernacle is literally an entire world of references, allusions and foreshadows of Christ and the church. One need not go very far to uncover the connections between Jesus and the Old Testament tabernacle — the New Testament reveals them to us. If you read about the Old Testament tabernacle in the light of the New Testament, you will never think the descriptions of the tabernacle and its furnishings are boring. Instead, you will be filled with hope and assurance, knowing that Jesus Christ, the true tabernacle, has come to redeem his people, living stones, and unite us to him, the one true foundation, so that we would become the eternal temple of the living God.

1
BUILDING MATERIALS

Read Exodus 25:1-9 (35:4-9)

Introduction

Whilst we are exploring the plans for the tabernacle, we must remember that we are looking at the shadows and types of the person and work of Christ. Jesus' relationship to the tabernacle is especially evident when he told his disciples, 'Something greater than the temple is here' (Matt. 12:6). But one of the most powerful statements Christ made was when he was walking through the Herodian temple complex and his disciples marvelled at the grandeur and immensity of the buildings. John tells us in his Gospel: 'Jesus answered them, "Destroy this temple, and in three days I will raise it up." The Jews then said, "It has taken forty-six years to build this temple, and will you raise it up in three days?" But he was speaking about the temple of his body' (John 2:19-21). We need to remember that Jesus is the ultimate embodiment of the temple — he is the chief cornerstone of the new temple, as the apostle Paul tells us in Ephesians (2:19-22).

This means that when we read of the tabernacle, we are looking at a shadowy picture of Christ and the church. We must keep this in mind, otherwise we might think that we are merely reading the instructions and account of the construction of a tent — and one to which the people of God have no connection. So let us turn to the first portion of the tabernacle, namely, the collection of the offerings for the tabernacle. As we reflect upon the narrative, we should pay particular attention to four things: first, the people gave of their possessions voluntarily and generously; second, Israel's offerings were for the construction of God's dwelling place; third, there was a good and bad use of the gold from Egypt; and, fourth, God was very specific regarding what materials were to be used in the construction of the tabernacle.

Instructions regarding the offering and materials

The initial instructions that Moses received were for contributions for the construction of the tabernacle. God told Moses to take up contributions, literally *offerings*, from the people. In other words, the people's offering was an act of worship. It was not merely a collection of needed materials, something like a trip to the local builders' merchants. What type of materials did God require for the tabernacle? It is obvious from the list that the very best types of materials were used, as they are listed in order of descending value: gold, silver and bronze (v. 3). God's plans also called for the use of blue, purple and scarlet yarns, which might not strike us as all that significant, especially in our own day when we can go to the local store and purchase yarn quite inexpensively.

When we consider, however, that twelve thousand murex snails were required to yield 1.4 grams of purple dye, all of a sudden the great value of these materials becomes evident. God also called for the use of fine linen, which undoubtedly came from Egypt, as with all of the precious materials Israel contributed towards the construction of the tabernacle. In addition to these materials, God's plans called for various types of animal skins, goats and rams, though some translations have porpoise (NAS) and sea cows

(NIV). The divine plans also called for precious stones, particularly for the high priest's breastpiece on his ephod.

To what end were all of these materials to be used? God wanted Moses to have the people construct a tabernacle or sanctuary so that God could 'dwell in their midst' (v. 8). We will see in upcoming chapters that God also gave Moses specific commands regarding the construction of the tabernacle — Moses was to follow the instructions down to the smallest detail (v. 9). He should follow God's instructions precisely, because the tabernacle was a copy of the heavenly temple. The author of Hebrews tells us: 'For Christ has entered, not into holy places made with hands, which are copies of the true things, but into heaven itself, now to appear in the presence of God on our behalf' (Heb. 9:24). So, then, when we look at the temple, we should realize that we are not only looking at a shadowy image of Christ and the church but we are, in a manner of speaking, looking at a piece of heaven on earth.

Reflecting upon the nature of the materials

As we reflect upon this passage of Scripture we should look at three features of the text that give us a better understanding of our connection to the passage and how we understand its significance in our own setting.

Voluntary offering

First, the offerings were not forced but were supposed to be voluntary. God told Moses to take an offering 'from every man whose heart moves him' (v. 2). In the parallel passage in Exodus 35 Moses tells the people, 'Whoever is of a generous heart, let him bring the Lord's contribution' (v. 5). In other words, the offerings were supposed to be a response from the people of God. The offerings were not repayment for their deliverance from Egypt, nor were they an effort to purchase their redemption — such thoughts are alien to the text. Rather, their giving towards the construction of the temple was supposed to be an act of heartfelt gratitude and worship.

Certainly Paul's instructions to the Corinthians echo God's instructions to Moses: 'Each one must give as he has made up his mind, not reluctantly or under compulsion, for God loves a cheerful giver' (2 Cor. 9:7). As we know, the people were not obedient because while Moses was at the top of Mount Sinai receiving these instructions, they were at the foot of the mountain plotting rebellion. The people eventually asked Aaron to fashion a graven image of God. Nevertheless, once God had dealt with their disobedience and Moses brought the request to the people, they responded in kind — and gave generously:

> 'The people bring much more than enough for doing the work that the LORD has commanded us to do.' So Moses gave command, and word was proclaimed throughout the camp, 'Let no man or woman do anything more for the contribution for the sanctuary.' So the people were restrained from bringing, for the material they had was sufficient to do all the work, and more
> (Exod. 36:5-7).

The people were told to stop giving because they had given more than enough for the construction of the tabernacle. Given the costly nature of the materials we see the depth of their generosity. Why did they give so generously? There are certainly many reasons, but one chief among them is that they were contributing to the construction of God's dwelling place.

Construction of God's dwelling place

Ever since the Garden of Eden the people of God had been alienated from their covenant Lord. God removed Adam and Eve from the presence of the garden, God's first earthly dwelling place, the first temple. When he removed them, and barred their access to his presence, he promised of a time when their fellowship would be restored, when the seed of the woman would conquer the seed of the serpent.

Israel's redemption from Egypt and now the construction of God's dwelling place in the midst of Israel was a giant step forward in restoring that broken fellowship. This restoration, the longing to dwell in the presence of God, I believe, was undoubtedly a motivating factor in the generosity of the Israelites. The psalmist expresses this sentiment well: 'I know that the LORD will maintain the cause of the afflicted, and will execute justice for the needy. Surely the righteous shall give thanks to your name; the upright shall dwell in your presence' (Ps. 140:12-13). Elsewhere the psalmist writes: 'For a day in your courts is better than a thousand elsewhere. I would rather be a doorkeeper in the house of my God than dwell in the tents of wickedness' (Ps. 84:10).

When we consider the generosity of the Israelites and the desire to dwell in the presence of the Lord, we should ask ourselves whether such behaviour marks us. In other words, are we generous in our giving? When we give our tithes and offerings, do we give generously knowing that it ultimately goes to the construction of the final dwelling place of God, the church? As the recipients of God's grace in Christ, do we give generously so that the gospel of Christ is preached in our own community, throughout our own country, and even throughout the world? As we know from the dominion mandate given to the first Adam, he was to fill the earth with the image of God and was supposed to extend the garden, the temple, to the ends of the earth. When Adam sinned, God himself took up the work he gave to Adam and told Abraham that through him all the nations would be blessed. God was going to accomplish the work of the dominion mandate — through his Son, the last Adam.

The last Adam took up the work of the mandate when he gave the church the Great Commission (Matt. 28:18-19). We are to go into every nation with the gospel; and the church cannot go into the nations apart from generous giving. The church, the people of God, must give generously so that the church, the final temple, the dwelling place of God, is built. There is another observation upon which we should meditate, namely, the source of the precious offerings.

Using Egypt's gold towards the right end

Israel as a nation of slaves had no wealth. When God delivered them from their cruel Egyptian overlords, he gave them favour with their masters; this divinely given favour enabled the Israelites to plunder them: 'And the LORD had given the people favour in the sight of the Egyptians, so that they let them have what they asked. Thus they plundered the Egyptians' (Exod. 12:36). But for Israel there was a good and bad use of the gold and treasures of Egypt. The good use was obviously for the construction of the house of God, the tabernacle. The bad use was the creation of the golden calf — a graven image of God (Exod. 32:4). I think there is an important lesson here, namely, how do we utilize our finances and possessions?

We can very easily turn the money we receive from our jobs and investments, and our possessions, into an idol, when God has given them to us so we can contribute to the construction of the temple, or the church. This, of course, casts a different light upon our employment. Do we go to work so we can make more money? And while the financial support of our families is definitely an important, noble and godly goal (1 Tim. 5:8), do we also have a desire to contribute more to the construction of the temple, the church? This passage should certainly cause us to think of our use of money — do we worship it, or use it to advance the gospel of

BUILDING MATERIALS

Christ? Last but not least, there is another element of this narrative that should draw our attention, namely, the specific instructions regarding what materials were to be used.

With what would the temple be built?

This narrative certainly highlights the specific kinds of materials that were supposed to be used to construct the tabernacle. In the New Testament Paul challenges the Corinthians regarding the nature of the materials they use for the construction of the church, the final temple:

> *According to the grace of God given to me, like a skilled master builder I laid a foundation, and someone else is building upon it. Let each one take care how he builds upon it. For no one can lay a foundation other than that which is laid, which is Jesus Christ. Now if anyone builds on the foundation with gold, silver, precious stones, wood, hay, straw — each one's work will become manifest, for the Day will disclose it, because it will be revealed by fire, and the fire will test what sort of work each one has done. If the work that anyone has built on the foundation survives, he will receive a reward. If anyone's work is burned up, he will suffer loss, though he himself will be saved, but only as through fire. Do you not know that you are God's temple and that God's Spirit dwells in you?*
> (1 Cor. 3:10-16).

Now to be sure, this passage is primarily directed at ministers and how they will build upon the foundation of the temple, namely Christ. Yet, at the same time, the questions that Paul poses are relevant to us all.

Will we construct the temple, the church, in accordance with the specific instructions that God has given? Will we construct it with the wisdom of man or with the materials that God has prescribed: the preaching and teaching of the Word, and Christ and him crucified; the administration of the sacraments, baptism and the Lord's Supper; and fervent prayer? We can only build upon the foundation of Christ with the materials that God has prescribed, nothing less will do. We should, therefore, like Moses, follow the commands of the Lord and use only those things he has ordained for the construction of the temple, the church.

Conclusion

As we read this narrative, remember the following four elements. First, the people gave of their possessions voluntarily and generously, therefore, by God's grace in Christ, give generously to the church. Second, Israel's offerings were for the construction of God's dwelling place, therefore as God's people, we who have been united to Christ, our great foundation, must pray that Christ would enable us to be faithful in spreading the gospel to all the nations of the earth so that God's dwelling place would be built through the preaching of the word. Third, there was a good and bad use of the gold of Egypt, therefore we ought to use the financial blessings that the Lord gives us, not as an idol, but to advance the gospel of Christ. Fourth, and last, God was very specific in what materials should be used for the tabernacle, therefore we must build the church with the specific materials that God has commanded: the Word, the sacraments and prayer.

2

THE ARK OF THE COVENANT

Read Exodus 25:10-22 (37:1-9)

Introduction

The popular movie *Raiders of the Lost Ark* portrays the Ark of the Covenant in such a way as to surround it in a shroud of mystery and attribute great powers to it. The truth of the matter is that there is no great mystery as to why the Ark of the Covenant was supposed to be very special. Rather than relying upon Hollywood for our theology, our understanding of the ark should be shaped by Scripture. The Bible should inform us why it has significance for Israel and for us as the people of God. Moreover, we should remember that the ark is significant because it points ultimately to the saving work of Jesus Christ.

The details of the ark

It is interesting that the instructions for the construction of the tabernacle begin, not with the actual tabernacle itself but the Ark of the Covenant. This is most likely so because the ark represented the supreme symbol of God's presence in Israel's midst after the exodus. We read in verse 10 that the ark was to be 2½ cubits in length (3 feet 9 inches) and 1½ cubits high (2 feet 3 three inches) and 1½ cubits wide. It was to be made out of acacia wood, the same wood to be used in the rest of the tabernacle and overlaid with gold. There were four rings (v. 12), two rings on each side of the ark, through which were to be placed two poles of wood. The poles were handles by which the Israelites were enabled to move and carry the ark, and they were never to be removed.

The function of the poles was to ensure that no human hands were ever to come in contact with the ark. We are reminded of the time when Uzzah was struck dead for touching the ark. The Israelites were transporting it on a cart, a practice Israel seems to have adopted from the Philistines, who had sent the ark back to the Israelites after they had captured it. They were transporting the ark when it hit a pothole; the ark was going to fall onto the ground so Uzzah reached out to steady it, touched it, and God struck him dead: 'And when they came to the threshing floor of Nacon, Uzzah put out his hand to the ark of God and took hold of it, for the oxen stumbled. And the anger of the Lord was kindled against Uzzah, and God struck him down there because of his error, and he died there beside the ark of God' (2 Sam. 6:6-7). The ark was God's throne and as such was sacred. No sinful human hands could therefore touch it, and if they did, judgement was swift and sure.

In verse 16 we read that Moses was to place the 'testimony' inside the ark. The 'testimony' is a synonym for 'the covenant', as the ark is called the 'ark of the testimony' (Exod. 40:21) as well as the 'ark of the covenant' (Num. 10:33). In other words, Moses was to place a copy of the Ten Commandments inside the ark. What is implicit here in Exodus is made explicit elsewhere: 'At that time the Lord said to me, "Cut for yourself two tablets of stone like the first, and come up to me on the mountain and make an ark of wood. And I will write on the tablets the words that were on the first tablets that you broke, and you shall put them in the ark"' (Deut. 10:1-2).

THE ARK OF THE COVENANT

Verse 17 informs us that on top of the ark was a cover, which the ESV calls 'a mercy seat'. The mercy seat, literally translated, means 'atonement covering'. In the Greek translation of the Old Testament (the Septuagint), the word used is the same as that which is rendered by the English term, 'propitiation'. For this reason the cover of the ark, or the mercy seat, has also been called propitiatory because of its connections with the Day of Atonement. The mercy seat was the primary place where the high priest was to make atonement for the sins of Israel, as Leviticus 16:12-16 elaborates in great detail. The high priest was supposed to bring a censer full of coals from the fire at the altar before the Lord's presence and carry it inside the holy of holies where the ark rested. The incense from the censer was a protective cloud that shielded the priest from looking directly upon the ark. The priest was then supposed to take some of the blood from a sacrificial bull and sprinkle it with his finger upon the mercy seat. Combining this with the sacrifice of a goat for a sin offering, the blood of which was to be sprinkled inside the veil of the holy of holies, the high priest thus made atonement for Israel's sins once a year.

In addition to the mercy seat, verse 18 shows that the Israelites were supposed to place two golden cherubim on top of the ark: 'The cherubim shall spread out their wings above, overshadowing the mercy seat with their wings, their faces one to another; towards the mercy seat shall the faces of the cherubim be' (Exod. 25:20). Once placed upon the top of the ark, God promised to meet with the Israelites, first with Moses and then with the subsequent high priests. From between the cherubim God would speak to his people and give them his commandments. Quite literally, the Ark of the Covenant, especially the mercy seat, was the throne of God on earth — heaven come down. We read in 1 Samuel: 'So the people sent to Shiloh and brought from there the ark of the covenant of the Lord of hosts, who is enthroned on the cherubim' (4:4). The psalmist also writes: 'The Lord reigns; let the peoples tremble!

He sits enthroned upon the cherubim; let the earth quake!' (Ps. 99:1). But the ark was not the only place where God maintained his throne.

In other portions of the Scriptures we find God's throne signalled by the presence of the cherubim. The first place God's throne appears is in the temple-garden of Eden. When man sinned, God drove the sin-defiled couple away from his presence, which was guarded by two cherubim with flaming swords, just like the two cherubim on top of the ark (Gen. 3:24). The throne-cherubim imagery later reappears in the prophet Ezekiel where he describes his call to his prophet office as the Lord opened the heavens to Ezekiel allowing him to peer into the throne room of God: 'And above the expanse over their heads there was the likeness of a throne, in appearance like sapphire; and seated above the likeness of a throne was a likeness with a human appearance' (Ezek. 1:26).

The most famous place where the cherubim and God's throne appears is the book of Revelation. When the apostle John was taken to heaven in his vision he beheld the throne of God, a throne surrounded by four living creatures, that is, four cherubim (Rev. 4:7). From this collection of passages, it is evident that the atonement cover, the mercy seat, was God's earthly throne. And, as we saw in the previous chapter, the ark is a copy of what exists in heaven, a copy of God's throne in the heavenly temple.

The ark in the light of the New Testament

Drawing near on the basis of the sacrifice of Christ

The connections to Christ and the church are clearly spelled out in the New Testament, particularly in the books of Romans and Hebrews. We already know of the strict instructions regarding how the ark was to be transported, as well as the commands concerning the Day of Atonement, that Israel had to take extreme care in dealing with and handling the ark. Why? Because it was the very throne of God. No one could approach the throne if they were defiled by sin.

Because all men are defiled by sin, only the high priest could approach the mercy seat, but only after purification rituals, making atonement for himself by slaughtering a bull, and then only by approaching the mercy seat with the blood of the sacrifice to make atonement for Israel's sins. Only through the sacrifice of Christ can we have the forgiveness of sins: 'For all have sinned and fall short of the glory of God, and are justified by his grace as a gift, through the redemption that is in Christ Jesus, whom God put forward as a propitiation by his blood, to be received by faith' (Rom. 3:23-25). The apostle John likewise writes that Jesus 'is the propitiation for our sins, and not for ours only but also for the sins of the whole world' (1 John 2:2).

But the clearest and most powerful connection between the Ark of the Covenant and Christ appear in the book of Hebrews in the ninth chapter. The author of Hebrews rehearses the procedures of the desert tabernacle in great detail, how in the first section of the tabernacle were the lampstand and the bread of presence. Beyond this initial section of the tabernacle was the holy of holies, the place where the Ark of the Covenant rested. Once the high priest had made his personal preparations for his own sin, he would enter the holy of holies to offer a sacrifice on behalf of the nation. However, the author of Hebrews also explains that these rituals and sacrifices ultimately did not remove sin but were only shadows of greater things to come, namely the ministry of our great high priest, Jesus Christ. Jesus did not enter a tent made with hands, he did not enter the earthly copy. Rather, he entered the heavenly temple, and not by the blood of bulls and goats, but by his own precious blood. Christ's blood alone brings cleansing, purification and the forgiveness of sins. For all of these reasons, the author of Hebrews writes: 'Therefore he is the mediator of a new covenant, so that those who are called may receive the promised eternal inheritance, since a death has occurred that redeems them from the transgressions committed under the first covenant' (Heb. 9:15). Christ's work as our great high priest supersedes the work of the Levitical priests who laboured under the Mosaic covenant.

In the light of Christ's sacrifice, we can enter into the presence of God without fear. We no longer have to depend upon the yearly sacrifice on the Day of Atonement. We are no longer restricted by the limitations of the high priest entering the holy of holies and sprinkling blood upon the mercy seat. Instead, we have Christ, our great high priest, who has entered the heavenly holy of holies and has shed his own precious blood so that we may enter the presence of God. The author of Hebrews therefore writes: 'Let us therefore come boldly to the throne of grace, that we may obtain mercy and find grace to help in time of need' (Heb. 4:16, NKJV). Through Christ and his sacrifice, we can obtain the grace of forgiveness and God's mercy. Christ is the propitiation for our sins: 'In this is love, not that we have loved God but that he loved us and sent his Son to be the propitiation for our sins' (1 John 4:10).

So, then, the ark was the place where Israel made atonement for their sins, which is now fulfilled by Christ in his sacrifice for us. There is also another element upon which we should meditate, namely, that the ark represented the presence of God, that he had taken up residence in Israel.

God's presence among his people

Christ was the ultimate manifestation of God's presence in the midst of his people. The apostle John tells us: 'And the Word became flesh and tabernacled among us' (John 1:14, my translation). Because

Christ has come, God no longer dwells in a tabernacle made with human hands but in the temple of his people: 'In him you also are being built together into a dwelling place for God by the Spirit' (Eph. 2:22). We, the church, both individually and corporately, are the final temple, the final dwelling place of God. Just as God placed the copy of the law within the ark within the tabernacle, so too he writes the law upon our hearts (Jer. 31:33-34). God places his law within our hearts, his dwelling place.

The imagery of God's dwelling presence appears at several key points in the book of Revelation. At the culmination of the seventh trumpet, John writes in Revelation of the opening of the heavens and the revelation of the heavenly temple in terms evocative of God's descent from Mount Sinai to dwell in the midst of his people in the tabernacle, as there was lightning, peals of thunder, the shaking of the earth (Rev. 11:15-19; *cf.* Exod. 20:18). But this glorious imagery also appears at the end of the book of Revelation when John saw the holy city, the new Jerusalem, descend out of heaven. John mixes two images that convey the spiritual bond that exists between his people, such as the city-temple described as a 'bride adorned for her husband'. On the heels of God's descent at the consummation of all things, John records a loud voice from the throne that said, 'Behold, the dwelling place of God is with man. He will dwell with them, and they will be his people, and God himself will be with them as their God' (Rev. 21:2-3). In terms evocative of the instructions for the construction of the ark, we read: 'No longer will there be anything accursed, but the throne of God and of the Lamb will be in it, and his servants will worship him' (Rev. 22:3).

In other words, the events at the foot of Sinai and the construction of the Ark of the Covenant looked forward to a time when God would dwell in the midst of his people, which we have begun to see fulfilled with Christ's first advent, which we currently enjoy by the work of the Holy Spirit who indwells us, and look forward to its ultimate fulfilment and culmination on the final day, when we physically dwell in the presence of the triune God.

Our connection

When we consider these things, we should rejoice because of the forgiveness of sins. We should marvel at the idea that now God no longer dwells in manmade structures but instead dwells within us because of the advent of Christ and the work of the Holy Spirit. But a crucial question is: Do we take for granted God's indwelling presence? Do we take for granted the forgiveness of sins? I think that familiarity can breed contempt — we quickly presume upon God's grace rather than treasure it and recognize that it is undeserved. We also fail, I believe, to marvel at the idea that when two or three are gathered together in prayer, Christ is in their midst and they are before the throne of God itself — the mercy seat. How much time, therefore, do we spend in prayer? I believe that the absence of prayer in our life is a failure to realize fully the significance of the truths presented before us in this text of Scripture.

Conclusion

My prayer is that we would all recognize the wonderful grace of God in how he has drawn near to us in his Son through the work of the Holy Spirit. I pray that we would read of the Ark of the Covenant, meditate upon it, and realize that we no longer sprinkle the blood of bulls and goats upon it but instead have the forgiveness of sins through the shed blood of Christ. I also hope that we would grow in our appreciation for prayer, drawing near to the throne of God, and even for corporate worship, the gathering together of the people of God, the temple of God.

3
THE TABLE AND THE BREAD OF PRESENCE

Read Exodus 25:23-30 (37:10-16)

Introduction

In the last chapter we explored the Ark of the Covenant and now we continue to consider the furnishings of the tabernacle. In this chapter we examine the table for the bread of presence. Perhaps we have heard of this table and are vaguely aware of its existence in the tabernacle, but beyond that, we know little about its function. Perhaps we have heard of the *show bread* but do not know why it was placed in the tabernacle. I hope that after this chapter we will have a greater understanding and appreciation of the table for the bread of presence. In so doing, we will see its connections to Christ and of course to us as the people of God.

The table and the show bread

In the instructions for the construction of the table, verse 23 states that the table was to be approximately three feet long, one and a half feet wide, and approximately two feet tall. The table was overlaid with pure gold, and was made out of acacia wood, the same type of wood that was used for the Ark of the Covenant. From the description, it appears as though the sole purpose of the table was to hold the bread of presence (v. 30). This table was to be placed in the inner tabernacle, not the holy of holies, but the room just outside the holy of holies. Verse 26 states that the table was to have four rings, two on each side, and two poles that went through the rings so the table could be carried like the Ark of the Covenant. In other words, the table was to be moved about like the ark; it was to be moved without sinful human hands actually touching the table.

Verse 29 tells us that the table was to be equipped with different kinds of dishes, all of which were to be made of pure gold. One kind of dish or plate was to be used for the bread of presence and frankincense, which we read of in Leviticus: 'You shall take fine flour and bake twelve loaves from it; two tenths of an ephah shall be in each loaf. And you shall set them in two piles, six in a pile, on the table of pure gold before the LORD. And you shall put pure frankincense on each pile, that it may go with the bread as a memorial portion as a food offering to the LORD' (Lev. 24:5-7).

There were other types of dishes: flagons (or pitchers) and bowls. According to verse 29, the pitcher, or flagon, was used to pour drink offerings into the bowls. The drink offering consisted of wine, though there is debate as to what purpose the drink offering served (Lev. 23:13). The Israelites were prohibited from pouring out a drink offering upon the altar outside of the tabernacle (Exod. 30:9). We also know that the high priest was only to sprinkle the blood of the sacrifice upon the mercy seat of the ark. In other words, it appears that the drink offering was placed on the table as a reminder, not that it was actually to be poured out upon any altar. The drink offering was likely to be consumed by the priests once a week.

THE TABLE AND THE BREAD OF PRESENCE

Not only were the priests, and only the priests, supposed to consume the wine of the drink offering but they were also supposed to eat the bread of the presence. God instructed the Israelites in Leviticus: 'Every Sabbath day Aaron shall arrange it before the LORD regularly; it is from the people of Israel as a covenant for ever. And it shall be for Aaron and his sons, and they shall eat it in a holy place, since it is for him a most holy portion out of the LORD's food offerings, a perpetual due' (Lev. 24:8-9). So, then, once a week on the Sabbath the priests were to eat the bread and drink the wine, and then set out a new pitcher of wine and freshly baked loaves of bread. You might remember the story of King David, when he was fleeing from Saul, how he came to the tabernacle and asked for food for himself and his companions, and the only food the priest had to offer was the bread of presence (1 Sam. 21:6).

Now the burning question is: What is the bread of presence? The term *bread of presence* is a little ambiguous, as it could mean simply the bread that is in the presence of God, or it could mean that God is in the bread. I think the former is the more likely answer — it is the bread that was in the presence of God. Remember that the Ark of the Covenant, the symbol and earthly throne of God, was only a few feet away behind the veil in the Holy of Holies. The bread, then, was not only to remind the Israelites, specifically the priests, of the presence of God just a few feet away but it was also to remind them of God's gracious provision for Israel. It did this in two chief ways.

First, remember that God ratified the Mosaic covenant (Exod. 24:11) by having the elders of Israel sit down in his presence and consume a meal. When the priests ate the bread and drank the wine in the tabernacle, it was a reminder of the covenant that God had made with the people. The bread was a reminder of Israel's redemption from Egypt as well as the ratification of the covenant on Mount Sinai. However, it was also a reminder of God's gracious provisions for Israel's physical needs.

Second, remember that when Israel first left Egypt they were in need of food and complained. God provided them with bread from heaven: 'Behold, I am about to rain bread from heaven for you, and the people shall go out and gather a day's portion every day, that I may test them, whether they will walk in my law or not' (Exod. 16:4). When God provided Israel with the bread from heaven, they were supposed to place some of the manna within the ark (Exod. 16:32-34). So then, the bread of presence was also likely a reminder of God's gracious provision for Israel's physical needs. Israel was hungry, and God fed them.

When we consider the table for the bread of presence, we also find another symbol that reminded Israel of God's nearness. The bread of presence also reminded Israel of their gracious covenant redemption and God's provision for Israel's every need, even feeding them when they were hungry.

The table and bread in the light of the New Testament

When we cross over in the New Testament to explore the connections between the table for the bread of presence and Christ, I think there are links at several places. There are connections with Christ's feeding of the five thousand, the Lord's Supper, and the Lord's Prayer.

Christ feeding the five thousand

I think the same elements that are connected to the bread of presence appear in Christ's feeding of the five thousand. When the crowds grew hungry, Christ took the five loaves and two fish from the boy, multiplied them, and provided for the physical sustenance of the crowd. Incidentally, whether there is an implied connection or not remains elusive, but there were twelve baskets of bread left over, the same number of loaves of bread on the table in the tabernacle. What is also of significance is how Christ explains the significance of the miracle of feeding the five thousand.

After Jesus withdrew from the crowd, some of the people followed him, and so he turned and told them: 'Truly, truly, I say to you, you are seeking me, not because you saw signs, but because you ate your fill of the loaves' (John 6:26). He then went on to explain that he was the true bread from heaven:

> *'Truly, truly, I say to you, it was not Moses who gave you the bread from heaven, but my Father gives you the true bread from heaven. For the bread of God is he who comes down from heaven and gives life to the world.' They said to him, 'Sir, give us this bread always.' Jesus said to them, 'I am the bread of life; whoever comes to me shall not hunger, and whoever believes in me shall never thirst'*
>
> (John 6:32-35).

This explanation of Jesus reveals clear connections between the manna and the bread of presence.

The tabernacle is a copy of the true tabernacle from heaven — the manna was from heaven, and by virtue of its presence in the tabernacle, the bread of presence was also bread from heaven. Christ identifies that he is the bread from heaven and the one who comes to him shall never hunger nor thirst. Just as the manna from heaven gave the Israelites life, and the covenant meal that the leaders ate in the presence of God also was a reminder of the life that God had given them in the exodus, so too anyone who believes in Christ receives life — eternal life.

The Lord's Supper

We certainly see the connections between Christ, the Lord's Supper, and the table for the bread of presence in the tabernacle. In Exodus 24 the elders of Israel ascended Mount Sinai to eat a covenant ratification meal in the presence of the Lord. Just prior to that meal Moses and the people of Israel ratified the Mosaic covenant and Moses sprinkled the sacrificial blood on the book of the covenant and over the people. These same elements appear, and uniquely so, in the Lord's Supper. In fact, one connecting feature between the two events is the phrase, 'the blood of the covenant'. This phrase only occurs in Exodus 24, the Gospel accounts of the Lord's Supper, and the ninth chapter of Hebrews. In the Lord's Supper, however, Christ ratified the new covenant with his own blood, not the blood of animals. Recall that the author of Hebrews connects the sacrifice of Christ, the blood of the covenant, with that which cleanses us from sin: 'Let us draw near with a true heart in full assurance of faith, with our hearts sprinkled clean from an evil conscience and our bodies washed with pure water' (Heb. 10:22).

Incidentally, some might wonder, upon what Old Testament practice is the Lord's Supper then based? Is not the Lord's Supper based on the Passover? Yes, the Lord's Supper is based upon the Passover, but at the same time there is often overlapping biblical practice and imagery from other Old Testament passages that point to the same aspect of Christ's work. For example, the Passover prefigures Christ's sacrifice, as do the Old Testament sacrifices on the Day of Atonement. Here there is overlap with the Passover and the bread of presence. We should also realize that the practices of the New Testament, such as the Lord's Supper, do not arise without precedent in the Old Testament. In other words, Christ did not invent the Lord's Supper but instead the supper has its precedence here with the bread of presence in the tabernacle.

We can think of the connections in this way: the Old Testament priests would gather in the tabernacle and consume the bread of presence and drink the wine — both of which pointed to God's

THE TABLE AND THE BREAD OF PRESENCE

gracious redemption and provision for his people. Likewise, the New Testament tells us that we are a royal priesthood, and we gather together to consume bread and wine as a covenant meal, as it is set apart and consecrated through prayer. The bread and wine, as we saw in Christ's explanation, points to our redemption in Christ. We read in John's Gospel:

> *Truly, truly, I say to you, unless you eat the flesh of the Son of Man and drink his blood, you have no life in you. Whoever feeds on my flesh and drinks my blood has eternal life, and I will raise him up on the last day. For my flesh is true food, and my blood is true drink. Whoever feeds on my flesh and drinks my blood abides in me, and I in him. As the living Father sent me, and I live because of the Father, so whoever feeds on me, he also will live because of me. This is the bread that came down from heaven, not as the fathers ate and died. Whoever feeds on this bread will live for ever*
> (John 6:53-58).

The point is this: when we celebrate the Lord's Supper, we commune and fellowship with our Lord Jesus Christ.

Just as the Old Testament priests who ate the bread and wine were reminded of God's presence just a few feet away in the holy of holies and were reminded of his gracious redemption, so too when we eat the Lord's Supper we are reminded of Christ's presence in our midst and of the redemption that we have through faith by his life, death and resurrection.

The Lord's Prayer

At the same time we are also reminded of how God provides for our spiritual and physical needs. Remember that the bread of presence was supposed to remind the Israelites of how God had provided for Israel's physical needs. It is most likely this connection that lies behind the famous statement in the Lord's Prayer: 'Give us this day our daily bread' (Matt. 6:11). This statement is also linked to the daily provision of the bread from heaven that the Lord gave Israel as they wandered in the wilderness until they entered the promised land. God therefore met the daily needs of his people far beyond what they could ever ask or imagine, and this was what the Old Testament priests were supposed to remember as they consumed the bread of presence.

Our connection through Christ

When we see the connections between the table, the bread of presence, and Christ, we are inevitably drawn to the connections to the church. As we can well imagine, the first important connection is ensuring that we look to Christ by faith. Do we realize that it is only through his shed blood that we have the forgiveness of sins? Do we realize that it is only by looking to Christ by faith, in his life, death, resurrection and ascension that we can possess eternal life? It is the reality of our redemption, then, that we celebrate in the Lord's Supper. Just as the Old Testament priests consumed the bread and the wine in the presence of God to remind them of their redemption, so too we fellowship with Christ in like manner when we, New Testaments priests, consume the bread and wine of the covenant meal in Christ's presence — he is present in the gathered body of the church.

These thoughts should cross our minds whenever we take the Lord's Supper. Like Israel, we should give thanks to God for our gracious covenant redemption through the sacrifice of Christ, our Passover lamb. At the same time, we should also be reminded of the daily bread that our heavenly Father gives to us. God provided for Israel's daily needs for food — he satisfied their hunger. How often do we take for granted so many of the creature comforts? I think we can easily do this because we see that many other people have the same things — food, homes, cars, clothes, money. Perhaps we get into the mindset that we possess these things because they are simply the consequence of our labours. We work, and then we buy and provide for our needs. Yet, if this passage reminds us of anything, it is that it is God who gives us our daily bread. We have jobs because God has been kind. We have clothes on our backs, money in the bank, roofs over our heads and food in our stomachs because God has graciously and over-abundantly provided for our needs.

Do we rise in the morning and grumble and mutter under our breath about how much we dislike our jobs? Do we complain because our house is not big enough, or the cars we drive not new enough? When we sit down to eat, do we begin to engorge ourselves giving little to any thought to the source of our meal? Perhaps in an agrarian society it was easier to be more grateful for a meal. For example, a farmer would have to till the soil, plant the seed, fertilize, water, and wait for the crop. Or the farmer would have to raise the calf, feed it, care for it, slaughter it, all before he could eat it. Naturally, agriculture and animal husbandry visually depend upon the providence of God — if there is no rain, then there are no crops. If there are no crops, then there is no food for man or animal. Just because we stroll down the aisle of our air-conditioned grocery store and load our shopping trolleys with food does not mean that we ought not to give thanks for our daily bread. Whether we sit for a meal, drive in our car, or go to work, we should give thanks to our gracious heavenly Father for providing us with our daily bread.

Conclusion

It is my prayer that as we continue to tour the tabernacle and its furniture we would learn to grow in appreciation for the person and work of Christ. In this case, that we would rejoice when we consume the Lord's Supper, remembering his life, death and resurrection, our redemption, fellowshipping with our Lord and Saviour and looking to him by faith alone. I also pray that we would give thanks for God's gracious daily provision for our every need. Indeed, we serve a gracious and loving covenant Lord who has given us our daily bread and the true bread from heaven, Jesus Christ.

4

THE LAMPSTAND AND OIL

Read Exodus 25:31-40 (37:17-24), and 27:20-21

Introduction

In the previous two chapters we examined the Ark of the Covenant and the table for the bread of presence. In this chapter we examine the golden lampstand and the oil for the lampstand. It does not seem immediately apparent as to why the instructions for the oil would be separated from the instructions for the lampstand. Nevertheless, I thought it prudent to treat the two passages together. As we explore this furnishing of the tabernacle, we need to remember that we are looking at shadow images of Christ and the church. Hopefully we will be able to see these connections more clearly after we examine this passage not only in its immediate context but also from the rest of Scripture.

The lampstand and oil

At the beginning of the passage, in verse 31, God tells the Israelites that they were to make a lampstand out of hammered gold. This was no lightweight lamp, as the lamp and its utensils were to be made out of a talent of gold (v. 39), which was about seventy-five pounds. The lampstand was to be placed on the south side of the inner room of the tabernacle, opposite the table for the bread of presence. Now, the lampstand does resemble what we now know as the *menorah*, a seven-lamped candle. However, we should not miss some of the important details that describe the lampstand.

We should note, for example, that the lampstand is shaped and designed to resemble a budding almond tree:

> *And there shall be six branches going out of its sides, three branches of the lampstand out of one side of it and three branches of the lampstand out of the other side of it; three cups made like almond blossoms, each with calyx and flower, on one branch, and three cups made like almond blossoms, each with calyx and flower, on the other branch — so for the six branches going out of the lampstand*
>
> (Exod. 25:32-33).

So, then, imagine the centre shaft of the lampstand, and coming out of each side were three branches that were shaped like the branches from an almond tree. On the end of each of the branches were almond blossoms, which had a calyx, a group of green leaves that surrounded the flower on the end. On the centre shaft of the lampstand, there were four cups shaped like almond blossoms (v. 34). There were supposed to be seven lamps, one light for each branch and one light on top of the center shaft. What about the oil for the lampstand?

The Israelites were supposed to use pure beaten olive oil for the lampstand (v. 20), which would provide virtually smoke-free bright light in the tabernacle. The lampstand was to be tended twice a day, morning and evening, which means that the lampstand was to stay perpetually lit throughout the night. The likely image portrayed in the perpetual illumination of the lampstand is that the priests

THE LAMPSTAND AND OIL

would be reminded of the glory that eternally emanates from the triune Lord (Ps. 104:1-2). As the light perpetually shone upon the table with the bread of presence, one loaf of bread for each of the twelve tribes, the priests would also be reminded that one day the people of God would dwell in the perpetual light of the peace-giving countenance of the face of God (Num. 6:24-26; 8:1-4).

The significance of the lampstand

As we can imagine, several questions surface regarding the lampstand and its significance. Why is the lampstand designed like an almond tree? Why are there seven lights on the lampstand? Why does the lampstand stay perpetually lit even through the night? There are no explicit answers to these questions, as the text does not reveal them. However, I think the rest of Scripture gives us some suggestions. We should realize, however, that what the Scriptures give us, I believe, is a great deal of overlapping imagery that is connected to the lampstand. There is no one image that exhausts the significance of the lampstand but, rather, they provide us with a pastiche or a collage of significance.

Why is the lampstand designed like an almond tree?

The lampstand is designed like an almond tree most likely to remind the Israelites of the Garden of Eden, and more particularly the tree of life. As we explore the tabernacle we are beginning to see items that draw our minds back to the garden, such as the cherubim over the Ark of the Covenant. The last time the cherubim appeared was at the gates of the Garden of Eden, guarding the approach to the tree of life. As the priests entered the tabernacle, they would be reminded of God's presence with the showbread, and seeing the tree-like lampstand, they would be reminded of God's presence in the first temple, the Garden of Eden. At the same time, however, the priests would be reminded of their sin, because just as the cherubim guarded the entrance to the garden, so too the cherubim guarded the entrance to the holy of holies.

Why are there seven lights on the lampstand?

We know from Scripture that the number *seven* is one of God's favourite numbers, so this certainly points us in the general direction as to why God had them make seven lights on the lampstand. Nevertheless, I think there are other immediate indicators as to why there are seven lights. One of the things that we will see in the next chapter is that the tabernacle is a miniature replica of the creation itself. If this is so, and this opinion is held by both Jewish and Christian interpreters, then there is a connection between the light of the lampstand and the light of the creation. The heavenly lights, the sun, moon and stars, were supposed to be signs for the seasons, days and years (Gen. 1:14). The time period marked by the lights of the creation were marked by sevens. The seventh day of the week was the Sabbath. The seventh month of the year was the month of atonement (Lev. 16:29). The seventh year was the sabbatical year, the forgiving of debts and freedom for slaves (Deut. 15). The seventh of the seven-year sabbaticals was the year of Jubilee (Lev. 25). Given this pattern of sevens, it seems fitting that the lampstand, a replica of the heavenly lights, would have seven lamps.

Why does the lampstand stay perpetually lit?

The answer to this question lies most likely in the being and attribute of God, as well as in his redemptive activity in the exodus. Remember, when the high priest entered the tabernacle he was immediately reminded that he was in the presence of God. Certainly the knowledge of the presence of the ark, God's throne on earth, resting just several feet away in the holy of holies would be on the priest's mind. The bread of presence would remind him of God's presence in the tabernacle. Likewise, God is said in the Scriptures to cover himself 'with light as with a garment' (Ps. 104:2). In other words, light emanates perpetually from the presence of God. Hints of this appear in God's redemptive activity in the exodus. God created the lights in the firmament, something the Israelites would have acknowledged seeing him defeat Pharaoh, the supposed incarnation of the sun god Ra. God likewise appeared as the cloud of fire that guided them through the night and protected them from the Egyptians when they fled Egypt (Exod. 13:21; 14:20-21). The priests, then, would be reminded of these attributes and activities of God as they entered the tabernacle and saw the lampstand burning perpetually, day and night.

The lampstand and oil in the light of the New Testament

Jesus as the true light

I think the first link between Christ and the lampstand appears in the connection between Christ and light. John writes in his Gospel: 'In him was life, and the life was the light of men. The light shines in the darkness, and the darkness has not overcome it' (John 1:4-5). Jesus also powerfully states: 'I am the light of the world. Whoever follows me will not walk in darkness, but will have the light of life' (John 8:12). We dwell in spiritual darkness and it is Christ, the light of the world, who gives us the ability to see, and illumines our path. So, then, as we reflect upon the lampstand of the tabernacle, our minds should be drawn to Christ as the true light, the one who redeems us from darkness.

If we are redeemed and are being conformed to the image of Christ, then this means that we are to reflect and shine forth the light of Christ before men. This is something that we read in Christ's Sermon on the Mount. Remember that Christ is called the light of the world, yet this is the same description Christ gives to his disciples: 'You are the light of the world. A city set on a hill cannot be hidden. Nor do people light a lamp and put it under a basket, but on a stand, and it gives light to all in the house. In the same way, let your light shine before others, so that they may see your good works and give glory to your Father who is in heaven' (Matt. 5:14-16).

The lampstand points to Christ and the church

We clearly see all of this imagery — light associated with the presence of God — the tabernacle (or temple), the lampstand, and the people of God shining forth the light of Christ all come together in the book of Revelation. The apostle John writes that when he first saw his vision he saw seven golden lampstands and one like the son of man, Jesus Christ, was standing in the midst of them. Jesus told John: 'Fear not, I am the first and the last, and the living one. I died, and behold I am alive for evermore, and I have the keys of Death and Hades' (Rev. 1:17-18). John then tells us the significance of the lampstands, in that they were 'seven churches' (Rev. 1:20).

Here John sees a vision of Christ in the heavenly temple, standing in the midst of seven lampstands. Christ holds seven stars in one hand, his face was shining like the sun, and he was tending to the seven lampstands. I believe we find the same collage of imagery that we saw with the lampstand in the tabernacle repeated here in Revelation. Notice that there is the presence of Christ, there is mention of the lampstands, the stars and the sun, and of course the setting is the heavenly temple bathed in the light of Christ. At the same time, notice that John identifies the lampstands as representing the seven churches to whom he was to write. So, then, as I said at the beginning of the chapter, we must always remember that when we look at the tabernacle we are looking at a shadow picture of Christ and the church.

THE LAMPSTAND AND OIL

In this case, the Bible itself clearly identifies the church with the lampstands. The picture in the book of Revelation is strikingly similar to the picture we see in the tabernacle in the book of Exodus. Just as the high priest, Aaron, would enter the tabernacle and tend the lampstand, seeing that it was illumined both night and day, here we see Christ tending to the seven lampstands, the church, seeing that they stay illumined with the light of his glory both night and day. What we must realize, however, is that we in the church are faced with a significant question, namely: Will we shine forth the light of the glory of Christ before the world?

Christ likened the good works of the church to the light of a lamp. Do we desire, then, to do good works, not so we can merit our salvation, nor to please men? Rather, do we desire to do good works, to be obedient to the law of God, so that the world around us sees the light of the glory of Christ? What will the world see when it peers into the church? Will it see sexual immorality, impurity, sensuality, idolatry, sorcery, enmity, strife, jealousy, fits of anger, rivalries, dissensions, divisions, envy, drunkenness, orgies, and the like, the works of the flesh (Gal. 5:19-21)? In many quarters of the church this is precisely what the world sees, for the church has been conformed to the patterns of this world rather than transformed by the renewing of their minds through the light of the gospel.

Instead, if we abide in Christ and the Spirit produces his fruit within us, then the world will look in the church and see love, joy, peace, patience, kindness, goodness, faithfulness, gentleness and self-control (Gal. 5:22-23). If our chief desire in life is to glorify God and enjoy him for ever, then our desire will be to shine forth the light of the glory of Christ before men by our good works. When we are insulted, we turn the other cheek. When we are disliked or hated, we respond in love. When we are faced with temptation, we flee. When we see others in need, we respond spiritually and physically, with prayer, love, comfort, and the provision of food, money and clothing. This is the light that Christ has called us to shine forth as a lampstand of his glory.

I cannot help but wonder whether the seven lights on the lamp, which reminded the Israelites of the time structure of the world — seven days, seven years, seven sabbatical years ending in Jubilee — is also captured in the church's activity. We, the church, the seven lampstands, continue to mark the passing of time as we gather together for worship in the presence of Christ each and every Lord's Day. Even in our regular worship if the church truly observed the Lord's Day, as a day dedicated solely to Christ, the world would take notice. At the same time, we should realize that Christ will not suffer churches who do not shine forth the light of his glory. Christ had John write a warning to the church at Ephesus: 'But I have this against you, that you have abandoned the love you had at first. Remember therefore from where you have fallen; repent, and do the works you did at first. If not, I will come to you and remove your lampstand from its place, unless you repent' (Rev. 2:4-5). Christ can and does remove those churches, those lampstands, that do not shine forth the light of his glory.

Conclusion

Our prayer should be that we would unceasingly shine forth the light of the glory of Christ before the world; and in so doing, that men would see our good works and praise God, that even unbelievers would see the light of the glory of Christ and turn to him in faith. There is, however, a message of hope buried in the passage before us.

Remember that the lampstand in the tabernacle was illumined both night and day, reminding the Israelites of the light of the glory from the presence of the Lord. Remember how the book of Revelation concludes: 'And I saw no temple in the city, for its

THE LAMPSTAND AND OIL

temple is the Lord God the Almighty and the Lamb. And the city has no need of sun or moon to shine on it, for the glory of God gives it light, and its lamp is the Lamb. By its light will the nations walk, and the kings of the earth will bring their glory into it, and its gates will never be shut by day — and there will be no night there' (Rev. 21:22-25). In the same way we should be filled with hope as we long for the consummation of all things, when we shall stand in the presence of the light of the glory of our triune Lord. For just as it was never dark in the tabernacle, so too it shall never be dark in the final temple, new Jerusalem, as we shall dwell eternally in the light of the glory of the Lord God Almighty and the Lamb.

5

THE TABERNACLE

Read Exodus 26:1-37 (36:8-38)

Introduction

We at last come to the instructions for the construction of the tabernacle itself. In the previous chapters we have examined the materials of the tabernacle, the Ark of the Covenant, the table for the bread of presence, and the golden lampstand. In this chapter we will examine the actual tabernacle, the tent, in which God dwelled in the midst of Israel. The tabernacle is yet another reminder of God's abiding presence in the midst of his people. He never abandoned Israel but was going to see them to their final destination, the land of promise, the fulfilment of God's covenant promise to Abraham, Isaac and Jacob.

What we must not forget is the connection between the tabernacle, Christ and the church. As we contemplate God's dwelling place on earth at this point in Israel's history, we will be reminded of God's abiding presence with his people. It is an important reminder to us, because all too frequently we allow the circumstances of life to drown out the truth that God always dwells in the midst of his people. God's abiding presence in Christ, especially, is an important truth and should be a great source of comfort to us all.

The tabernacle

The inner curtain (vv. 1-6)

In verses 1-6 God gives instruction for the manufacture of ten curtains that were to be woven out of expensive fabric. These ten curtains were to be paired to make five sets of double-curtains — the sets of curtains were supposed to be joined by fifty loops on each end-curtain and fifty gold fasteners to form one continuous length of fabric. The one piece of fabric was to be approximately 60 feet long and 42 feet high, from top to bottom.

The outer curtain (vv. 7-14)

To protect the inner layer of the tabernacle, the Israelites were supposed to fashion an outer protective layer made from goatskin. This second layer was to protect the expensive inner layer from the elements, whether wind, sun, rain, dust etc.

The frames (vv. 15-25)

The curtains that we have seen described in verses 1-14 were to be held in place by a series of frames, or what we can call 'tent frames'. They were a series of upright supports that were to be placed in pedestals made out of silver, and joined together by cross-beams. The frames were to be made out of acacia wood, as were the other furnishings of the tabernacle, and overlaid with gold. The supports were to be approximately 15 feet tall and about 2 feet wide.

Cross beams (vv. 26-30)

There were a series of cross beams that were to be constructed in similar fashion to the frames of verses 15-25. These cross beams were to be joined to the frames and, once connected, would form

THE TABERNACLE

the rectangular tabernacle, upon which the inner and outer curtains would be hung. Like a modern-day tent, this type of construction lent itself to portability.

The layout of the tabernacle (vv. 31-37)

In this portion of the text God gives to Israel the basic layout of the tabernacle. The tabernacle was to have the most holy place, or what we would know as the holy of holies, where the Israelites were to place the Ark of the Covenant. Separating the holy of holies was a blue curtain with embroidered cherubim on it. In the room just outside the holy of holies was the altar of incense, the table for the bread of presence, on the north; and the golden lampstand on the south.

Purpose and significance

Having considered its dimensions and the nature of its construction, what was the purpose and significance of the tabernacle? Remember back to the first narrative describing the instructions for the tabernacle. The Israelites were supposed to construct this tabernacle so God could dwell in this midst of his people: 'And let them make me a sanctuary, that I may dwell in their midst' (Exod. 25:8). Quite literally the tabernacle was to be a visual reminder that God was with his people, that he was 'Immanuel' (Matt. 1:23).

In fact, at the conclusion of the construction of the tabernacle God's presence settled upon the tabernacle in the form of a pillar of cloud by day and a pillar of fire by night: 'On the day that the tabernacle was set up, the cloud covered the tabernacle, the tent of the testimony. And at evening it was over the tabernacle like the appearance of fire until morning. So it was always: the cloud covered it by day and the appearance of fire by night' (Num. 9:15-16). So, then, we certainly see the significance of the tabernacle

51

in this regard — the tabernacle was a visible reminder of God's presence in their midst. We should also remember, however, that the tabernacle was a copy of the heavenly temple.

Let us consider, first, several things about the very creation itself. We should recognize that the Bible likens the entire creation to a temple for God. The psalmist writes that God covers himself with light as with a garment and stretches out the heavens like a tent covering (Ps. 104:2). The prophet Isaiah observes: 'It is he who sits above the circle of the earth, and its inhabitants are like grasshoppers; who stretches out the heavens like a curtain, and spreads them like a tent to dwell in' (Isa. 40:22). Again, Isaiah states: 'Thus says the LORD: "Heaven is my throne, and the earth is my footstool; what is the house that you would build for me, and what is the place of my rest"' (Isa. 66:1).

Given these statements from Scripture, commentators explain that this is why the tabernacle's inner curtain is blue — to resemble the sky. The veil that separates the holy of holies from the rest of the tabernacle was also supposed to be blue. If you recall that when Ezekiel saw that throne of God in his vision, he looked up into the sky and saw cherubim, and above the cherubim he saw the throne of God (Ezek. 1). This is the same idea that appears with the blue curtain that divides the holy of holies from the rest of the tabernacle. Moreover, as we will see in the upcoming chapters, there was also a bronze laver outside the tabernacle, which was essentially a large washbasin. Scholars connect this bronze laver with the body of water that sits before the throne of God in heaven, the glass sea (*cf.* Rev. 4). This pattern is also reproduced in the creation, as man was to rule from the dry earth, which of course sits by the waters.

We also saw in the previous chapter how the golden lampstand was connected to the lights of the cosmos, the sun, moon and stars. We can conclude, therefore, that the creation itself is a macrocosmic temple and that the tabernacle is a microcosmic temple, a miniature version of the heavens and earth. In fact, it was the Jewish historian, Josephus, who said that the tabernacle was 'made in way of imitation and representation of the universe' (Antiquities 3.180). We need to keep these things in mind as we cross over into the New Testament and consider the significance of the tabernacle in the light of the revelation of Christ.

The tabernacle in the light of the New Testament

We should recognize the immediate connection between Christ and the tabernacle. The tabernacle was the visible sign of God's presence in the midst of his people. The apostle John takes up this very tabernacle imagery in the opening chapter of his Gospel: 'And the Word became flesh and tabernacled among us, and we have seen his glory, glory as of the only Son from the Father, full of grace and truth' (John 1:14, translation mine). Just as the glory cloud descended upon the tabernacle, so too Christ, Immanuel, tabernacled in the midst of God's people; and his glory, the glory of the triune Lord, rested upon him as it did upon the desert tabernacle. God no longer tabernacled among his people in a tent but rather in human flesh and bones — Jesus Christ is fully God but also fully man.

The same theme, the indwelling presence of God, appears in the events at Pentecost. First, recall that we are the temple of God, the final dwelling place of our triune Lord. Christ, of course, is the chief cornerstone: 'So then you are no longer strangers and aliens, but you are fellow citizens with the saints and members of the household of God, built on the foundation of the apostles and prophets, Christ Jesus himself being the cornerstone, in whom the whole structure, being joined together, grows into a holy temple in the Lord. In him you also are being built together into a dwelling place for God by the Spirit' (Eph. 2:19-22). So, then, we are indwelt by the presence of the Holy Spirit.

But, second, recall when the Holy Spirit first settled upon the church at Pentecost: 'And suddenly there came from heaven a sound like a mighty rushing wind, and it filled the entire house where they were sitting. And divided tongues as of fire appeared to them and rested on each one of them. And they were all filled with the Holy Spirit and began to speak in other tongues as the Spirit gave them utterance' (Acts 2:2-4). Just as the pillar of cloud and fire rested over the desert tabernacle, fire rested over the disciples, indicating that they, as the temple of God, now had the presence of the Holy Spirit, the very presence of God himself dwelling within them.

When we contemplate the tabernacle, we should meditate upon the abiding presence of God with his people. Remember that God tabernacled in the midst of Israel — he dwelled in a tent because he accompanied his people on their journey to the promised land. He had given them his promise and word that he would bring them into their final earthly resting place, the land that God had promised to give Abraham, Isaac and Jacob. He did not abandon his people, even when they made repeated attempts to abandon him. There, in the middle of Israel's camp, God dwelled in the tabernacle, accompanying, protecting and guiding his people. The same may be said of God's presence in the midst of his people even now in our own day. God came in the person of his Son, Jesus Christ, and tabernacled in the midst of his people. And now, Christ continues to tabernacle in the midst of his people by the person and work of the Holy Spirit. Christ dwells in the hearts of his people. And, just as God accompanied Israel to the promised land as he tabernacled in their midst, so too Christ tabernacles in our midst by the indwelling presence of the Holy Spirit. The big difference, of course, is that God no longer dwells in a manmade tent but instead in us!

He is faithfully seeing us to our destination — the true promised land — to Mount Zion itself, to heaven. This means that we are never alone! There may come times when we feel alone, when it seems as though Christ is nowhere to be found. Yet, we know from the shadow of the tabernacle and the advent of Christ that we should not let the truth of Scripture, the abiding presence of Christ among his people, be drowned out by our doubts and fears. Remember the promise of Christ: 'Go therefore and make disciples of all nations, baptizing them in the name of the Father and of the Son and of the Holy Spirit, teaching them to observe all that I have commanded you. And behold, I am with you always, to the end of the age' (Matt. 28:19-20).

So, then, when we feel as though we cannot find Christ, perhaps due to depression, stress, fear or anxiety, then let us draw nigh to Christ — let us acknowledge that Christ is at hand. Pick up the Word of God and read it — for Christ speaks to us through it. The Word reminds us that Christ is not far off but within our hearts. Therefore we should drop to our knees in prayer — for we have access to the throne of God. Be assured that Christ will never leave us, never forsake us, but will always dwell within his tabernacle, the church, by the power of the Holy Spirit. We do have an even greater hope to which we can look forward.

Conclusion

As we read of the construction of the tabernacle and then the incarnation of Christ, and his indwelling presence within us, we must live by faith. We cannot see Christ and sometimes, unfortunately, our fears and doubts get the better of us, if only for a time. Nevertheless, we have the wonderful hope of the coming new heavens and earth:

> *Then I saw a new heaven and a new earth, for the first heaven and the first earth had passed away, and the sea was no more. And I saw the holy city, new Jerusalem, coming down out of heaven from God, prepared as a bride adorned for her husband. And I heard a loud voice from the throne saying, 'Behold, the dwelling place of God is with man. He will dwell with them, and they will be his people, and God himself will be with them as their God. He will wipe away every tear from their eyes, and death shall be no more, neither shall there be mourning nor crying nor pain anymore, for the former things have passed away'*
>
> (Rev. 21:1-4).

We can look forward to the day when faith will give way to sight. Christ will not only indwell us spiritually but we will dwell for all eternity in the presence of our triune Lord. We will behold the face of God in Christ. Then our fellowship will be complete, we will know completely and fully what Israel only knew in shadows and in a manmade tent, and what we now know in the power of the Spirit — the eternal abiding presence of God. Indeed, then we will completely and fully know the meaning of Immanuel, God with us.

6

THE ALTAR AND COURTYARD

Read Exodus 27:1-19 (38:1-7, 9-20)

Introduction

Thus far we have explored the significance of the Ark of the Covenant, the table for the bread of presence, the golden lampstand, and the tabernacle itself. In this chapter we explore the altar for burnt offerings and the outer courtyard. God dwelled in the midst of Israel, which was an honour and privilege for the people of God. Access to God's presence, however, was an entirely different matter. As we will see from our study of the altar, the first thing to confront the one who entered the confines of the tabernacle was the altar for burnt offerings. This, as we can well imagine, sent an important message to those who wanted to be in the presence of God. And, as we will see when we explore the significance of the altar from the New Testament, there are connections to Christ and the church.

The courtyard and altar

The outer courtyard (27:9-19)

As we saw in the previous chapter, God gave the Israelites instructions for the fabrication of the tabernacle proper. The tabernacle itself, however, did not simply sit in the midst of Israel allowing anyone to approach. Rather, the tabernacle was surrounded by an outer courtyard that was approximately 150 feet by 75 feet, enclosed by white linen hangings, a wall of linen if you will, that was 7½ feet tall. This outer courtyard separated Israel from the actual tabernacle. On the east side of the tabernacle, there was a gate through which the people could enter. But the very first thing the Israelites would see as they entered the gate of the courtyard was the altar for burnt offerings.

Altar for burnt offerings (27:1-8)

The altar was a square made out of acacia wood, like the rest of the tabernacle, though it was covered in bronze, not gold. Scholars argue, and rightly so, that the further away from the holy of holies you were, the lesser were the values of the metals that were used. In the holy of holies and inner tabernacle, everything was covered in gold, which was to symbolize the glory and immediate presence of God, and to remind the Israelites of the heavenly tabernacle. The outer courtyard, however, was a symbolic representation of the earth, hence lesser metals such as bronze, copper and silver were used in these portions of the tabernacle.

The altar was five cubits square, or approximately 7½ feet square, and 4½ feet tall. It was hollow in the middle and most likely filled with uncut stones and earth. On the top of the altar there was a grate made out of bronze — it is on top of this grate that the burnt offerings were placed. There were also four protruding corners of the altar that God calls the 'horns' of the altar (Exod. 27:2). And, like the rest of the tabernacle, the altar was built for portability, in that God directed the Israelites to fabricate wooden poles to insert in four rings on the corners of the altar. This way the altar could be carried like the ark and the table for the bread of presence. God also instructed the Israelites to fabricate tools to use with the altar:

buckets to carry the ashes away from the altar; shovels to scoop the ashes out of the altar; and forks and fire pans for handling the sacrifices that were to be placed on the altar. What were the Israelites required to do with the altar?

Burnt offerings (Lev. 4:2-21)

The book of Leviticus tells us that the Israelites used the altar to make sin offerings. Israel and the high priest did not have access to God whenever they wanted but could only approach under the blood of a burnt offering, a sacrifice for their sin. The high priest would bring a bull without blemish and slaughter it at the entrance, the courtyard of the tabernacle (Lev. 4:4). He would then take some of the blood and sprinkle it seven times on the veil separating the holy of holies from the inner tabernacle (Lev. 4:5-6). The priest then took some of the blood and placed it on the four horns of the altar and then poured out the rest of the blood at the base of the altar (Lev. 4:7). He then took the fat, kidneys, loins and liver, and burned them all upon the altar (Lev. 4:8-10). He then took the rest of the bull — its flesh, head, legs, entrails, and dung — and burnt it outside the camp (Lev. 4:11-12).

The symbolism in the burnt offering is powerful, as we can well imagine. The imagery is certainly substitutionary, in that the one who sinned would offer an animal in his own place to appease the wrath of God and receive the forgiveness of his sins. There was an emphasis upon the shedding of blood, because we know from other portions of Scripture that the blood was identified with the life of a creature (*cf.* Gen. 9:4):

> 'For the life of the flesh is in the blood, and I have given it for you on the altar to make atonement for your souls, for it is the blood that makes atonement by the life ... For the life of every creature is its blood: its blood is its life. Therefore I have said to

the people of Israel, You shall not eat the blood of any creature, for the life of every creature is its blood. Whoever eats it shall be cut off'

(Lev. 17:11, 14).

Israel was supposed to sacrifice and smear blood on the horns of the altar, for the consecration of priests (Exod. 29:12), for sin offerings (Lev. 4:25, 30), and on the day of atonement (Lev. 16:18).

One thing should emerge quite clearly from all of the information we have gathered — namely, there was a constant reminder of God's holiness and man's sinfulness at the entrance to the tabernacle courtyard. Israel would have a blunt reminder of the cost of the forgiveness of sins as they saw and heard a bull slaughtered, saw the blood smeared upon the horns of the altar, smelled the burning fat, and then carried the remains of the animal outside of the camp to be burned. The Israelites would know from the gruesome ritual that sin was costly, but at the same time would also know they served a God who was willing to forgive their transgressions. Indeed, the Israelites would know that the horns of the altar were a place of refuge and shelter. Recall that when Joab, one of King David's trusted advisors, supported the rise of Adonijah as king rather than David's choice of Solomon, he fled to the tabernacle and grabbed hold of the horns of the altar, a symbolic action of his desire to find the mercy of God (1 Kings 2:28-34).

The altar in the light of the New Testament

The connections to Christ

The sacrifices of the Old Testament foreshadow and point forward to the perfect sacrifice of Jesus Christ. The author of Hebrews, probably more so than any other in the New Testament, makes the explicit connection between the sacrifices of the Old Testament

THE ALTAR AND COURTYARD

and the sacrifice of Christ:

> *These preparations having thus been made, the priests go regularly into the first section, performing their ritual duties, but into the second only the high priest goes, and he but once a year, and not without taking blood, which he offers for himself and for the unintentional sins of the people. By this the Holy Spirit indicates that the way into the holy places is not yet opened as long as the first section is still standing (which is symbolic for the present age). According to this arrangement, gifts and sacrifices are offered that cannot perfect the conscience of the worshipper, but deal only with food and drink and various washings, regulations for the body imposed until the time of reformation*
> (Heb. 9:6-10).

Notice that verses 6-7 address the elements of the sacrifices that we have explored in our study of the altar.

What is particularly of interest is the significance the author gives to the very structure of the tabernacle, showing us that it is replete with symbolic meaning. The author says in verse 8 that the way into the heavenly holy of holies was not yet opened as long as the first section was standing, namely, the veil separating the holy of holies from the rest of the tabernacle. The author states that the veil that separated the holy of holies from the rest of the temple was 'symbolic for the present age' (v. 9a). In other words, with the fall of Adam and the entrance of sin into the world, the way to access and fellowship with God was obstructed. The tabernacle was a symbolic representation of what would happen in the future, namely, that one would make a sacrifice, opening the way once again to the presence of God. Symbolically, once a year, the high priest would enter by the shed blood of the sacrifice, opening the veil and entering the holy of holies.

CHRIST AND THE DESERT TABERNACLE

Now that Christ, the true high priest, has come, he has done precisely what was foreshadowed in the Old Testament sacrifice of the burnt offering upon the altar:

> *But when Christ appeared as a high priest of the good things that have come, then through the greater and more perfect tent (not made with hands, that is, not of this creation) he entered once for all into the holy places, not by means of the blood of goats and calves but by means of his own blood, thus securing an eternal redemption*
>
> (Heb. 9:11-12).

Christ entered the heavenly holy of holies and offered a sacrifice with his own blood by which he secured our redemption. There are still further connections between Christ's sacrifice and the burnt offerings upon the altar. The blood from the animals was smeared upon the horns of the altar, sprinkled upon the veil between the holy of holies and the inner tabernacle, and also upon the mercy seat. Remember, though, what happened with the rest of the animal: its fat was burned upon the altar.

I believe burning the fat was symbolically connected to the wrath of God, as throughout Scripture we see fire connected with God's judgement. We certainly know that Christ bore the wrath of the Father upon the cross. Also recall that the remains of the animal, the head, legs, entrails and dung, were carried outside the camp and burned as well. This aspect of the burnt offering is also captured in Christ's crucifixion: 'For the bodies of those animals whose blood is brought into the holy places by the high priest as a sacrifice for sin are burned outside the camp. So Jesus also suffered outside the gate in order to sanctify the people through his own blood' (Heb. 13:11-12). Jesus was crucified outside Jerusalem, outside the camp. Burning the sacrificial animal outside the camp symbolically pictured that the sins of the one who brought the sacrifice had been taken away, burned and forgotten. The same may be said of the sacrifice of Christ — he was sacrificed outside the camp so that he might sanctify the people of God with his own blood.

The connections to the church

The connections between the altar for burnt offerings and the church are clear, especially in the light of Christ. Unlike Israel, we are no longer confronted with the altar every time we enter the confines of the tabernacle. Rather, Christ offered himself as a perfect sacrifice once and for all, and now, what was only symbolically portrayed in Israel's sacrifices upon the altar has been fulfilled by Christ. We now have access to the very presence of God — we have access to the throne of grace through the sacrifice of Jesus Christ and his shed blood. There are no longer sacrifices year after year, sin after sin, but the once-for-all sacrifice of Jesus Christ has come, which brings atonement for sins, past, present and future.

There is therefore the important connection between the altar and the church through the sacrifice of Christ.

> *Consequently, when Christ came into the world, he said, 'Sacrifices and offerings you have not desired, but a body have you prepared for me; in burnt offerings and sin offerings you have taken no pleasure. Then I said, "Behold, I have come to do your will, O God, as it is written of me in the scroll of the book."' When he said above, 'You have neither desired nor taken pleasure in sacrifices and offerings and burnt offerings and sin offerings' (these are offered according to the law), then he added, 'Behold, I have come to do your will.' He abolishes the first in order to establish the second. And by that will we have been sanctified through the offering of the body of Jesus Christ once for all. And every priest stands daily at his service, offering repeatedly the same sacrifices, which can never take*

> *away sins. But when Christ had offered for all time a single sacrifice for sins, he sat down at the right hand of God, waiting from that time until his enemies should be made a footstool for his feet. For by a single offering he has perfected for all time those who are being sanctified*
>
> (Heb. 10:5-14).

One of the questions that we should ask ourselves is: Do we fully realize the significance of the once-for-all sacrifice of Christ?

So often we will give lip service to the idea of the sacrifice of Christ, but our conduct reveals our lack of understanding in our hearts. Many claim to take refuge in the sacrifice of Christ, but they live in rebellion to the authority of Christ — they claim to love Christ but their lives demonstrate they are indifferent to the costly sacrifice of Jesus Christ. There are still yet others who claim the name of Christ and look to him for the forgiveness of sins, yet they live as though we still worshipped at the Old Testament tabernacle. In other words, they believe that their sin is too great for God to forgive, and so, like the Old Testament Israelites, they repeatedly come to God doubting his mercy and seek the forgiveness of a sin, offering their prayers and repeatedly pleading with God for forgiveness for the same one sin over and over again.

Oddly enough, both types of sin are manifestations of pride — the former thinks too much of himself, which is arrogance, because he does not believe he needs the forgiveness of sins. The latter thinks too much of his sin and too little of the sacrifice of Christ, because Christ could never forgive him, or so he thinks. We should occupy neither of these positions of arrogance and pride.

We should recall the costly sacrifice of Christ and rejoice that we can envision the horns of the altar smeared with blood, cling to them in Christ, and know that our sins accuse us no more. If Christ gave his life so that we might live, then we must not live as though Christ never came, as though he never offered himself up on our behalf. We must, as Paul says, walk in the newness of life, for our sinful nature has been crucified with Christ: 'Those who belong to Christ Jesus have crucified the flesh with its passions and desires' (Gal. 5:24).

At the same time, when we fall into sin, even grievous sin, we are not beyond forgiveness. Do not think that we can somehow atone for our sins if we ask God to forgive us many times. We should rest assured and rejoice that when we ask for God's forgiveness we have it because of the sacrifice of Christ. As the psalmist says, 'As far as the east is from the west, so far does he remove our transgressions from us' (Ps. 103:12). Rejoice, knowing that your heavenly Father forgives you on account of the perfect sacrifice of Christ.

Conclusion

When in our mind's eye we enter the confines of the tabernacle as the ancient Israelites did so many thousands of years ago, let our gaze fall upon the person and work of Christ. Remember that he is the perfect sacrifice, the one who has secured our redemption. Remember that Christ has torn the veil in two and that we can once again enter into the presence of our holy and righteous God.

7

THE PRIEST'S GARMENTS

Read Exodus 28:1-43 (39:1-31)

Introduction

We have explored the various aspects of the tabernacle, the contributions of materials, the Ark of the Covenant, the table for the show bread, the golden lampstand, the tabernacle itself, the bronze altar and outer courtyard. At this point we take a diversion from the actual tabernacle and its furnishings to explore the instructions regarding the clothing of the priests, and more specifically the clothing for the high priest. Though God dwelled in the midst of Israel, the people could not approach God's presence in any manner they saw fit. Rather, just as there were ritual sacrifices that had to be performed to enter God's presence, such as the burnt offerings, so too the priests, especially the high priest, had to be clothed in specific garments. We will explore the nature of these garments and examine their connection to Christ and the church. In so doing we will see that we, as priests of God, are clothed with special garments just as Aaron was clothed.

CHRIST AND THE DESERT TABERNACLE

The priest's garments

Holy garments for Aaron (vv. 1-5)

God begins this portion of the chapter by telling Moses that Aaron and his sons, Nadab and Abihu, were to serve as priests for the people. They were to be the representatives of the people in the presence of God. They were to be clothed, however, in 'holy garments' which are to be 'for glory and for beauty' (v. 2). The garments were supposed to be made out of the same materials as the tabernacle: gold, blue, purple and scarlet yarns, and fine twined linen (v. 5).

The ephod (vv. 6-14)

In theses verses we find the description of the ephod, which was similar to a robe made out of fine linen. We are left in the dark as to exactly what the ephod looked like, though it had four parts: the main part of the garment, two shoulder pieces, and an elaborate belt. The two shoulder pieces were supposed to have an onyx stone mounted on each one with the names of the twelve tribes of Israel engraved upon them in order of their birth. While the text does not specifically state it, the idea seems to be that the high priest would representatively carry the twelve tribes of Israel into the tabernacle and holy of holies. The tribes were, in a sense, upon the shoulders of the priest.

The breastpiece of judgement (vv. 15-30)

The breastpiece was something like a shield that was worn over the chest. It was a perfect square, nine inches by nine inches, and had four rows of precious stones placed upon it, with three stones in each row. This represented one stone for each of the twelve tribes of Israel, and each stone had the name of a tribe engraved upon it. The idea is that the high priest represents the people of God and carries them with him into the holy of holies, into the presence of God.

At this point we should realize that the priest is essentially wearing a miniature replica of the tabernacle. His garments reproduce the tabernacle, as they are made out of the same material, and the perfect square upon his chest represents the holy of holies. Remember that in the Solomonic temple the holy of holies was a perfect cube. There, God said what he would do from above the mercy seat in the holy of holies: 'There I will meet with you, and from above the mercy seat, from between the two cherubim that are on the ark of the testimony, I will speak with you about all that I will give you in commandment for the people of Israel' (Exod. 25:22). God would render his judgements and give commandments for the people; that is, reveal his will. In similar fashion, therefore, Aaron was to place the Urim and Thummim, which were for casting lots, that is, revealing the will of God for making decisions: 'And in the breastpiece of judgement you shall put the Urim and the Thummim, and they shall be on Aaron's heart, when he goes in before the Lord. Thus Aaron shall bear the judgement of the people of Israel on his heart before the Lord regularly' (Exod. 28:30).

The robe (vv. 31-35)

The next item of clothing to be worn is the robe of the priest. This robe is called the 'robe of the ephod', which indicates that the robe was to be worn under the ephod and breastpiece. The robe was to be made out of the same materials used in the tabernacle, and had openings for the head and arms, and was to be put on like a sweater. The robe was decorated with embroidered pomegranates, which were symbolic of God's fruitfulness, reminding us of the Garden of Eden. Recall that the spies brought back pomegranates from their reconnaissance of the promised land (Num. 13:23), a land flowing with milk and honey, imagery evocative of the pristine and fecund Garden of Eden. Additionally, the walls of the Solomonic temple were adorned with bronze pomegranates. The overall intent is that the priest was wearing a replica of the tabernacle, in a sense conveying that the priest himself was a part of the tabernacle.

Upon the hem of this robe the Israelites were to attach bells: 'And it shall be on Aaron when he ministers, and its sound shall be heard when he goes into the Holy Place before the LORD, and when he comes out, so that he does not die' (Exod. 28:35). These bells were necessary to keep the high priest alive — he could not enter the holy of holies without them. As to the precise function of the bells, we cannot be sure, though there are some suggestions. One such suggestion is that the noise that came from the bells was to remind the priest of his duties and his ministrations before the presence of the Lord. Others have suggested that the bells would also let those outside the holy of holies know that the high priest was still alive, because they dare not enter the holy of holies to check.

The head plate (vv. 36-38)

Aaron was supposed to wear a turban on his head, and on the turban was a gold plate with the words 'Holy to the Lord' engraved upon it. Given Aaron's function to represent Israel as a nation, not only does this head plate remind Aaron that he was holy, set apart to the Lord and his service, but that Israel as a nation was set apart as well. Recall that God told the Israelites that they were to be a 'kingdom of priests and a holy nation' (Exod. 19:6).

Linen coat (v. 39)

Aaron was supposed to wear a coat woven out of fine linen, one that bore a chequered pattern, and the turban was to be made of the same material. There was also a sash, or a belt, apparently to secure the fine linen coat. So, then, it appears that Aaron would first put on the fine linen coat, which seems to be an undergarment, and the turban. He would then don the robe, followed by the ephod and the breastpiece of judgement.

Garments for Aaron's sons (vv. 40-43)

Lastly, the other priests were to be clothed in a similar fashion to the high priest, though not in precisely the same clothing. They were also to wear linen undergarments, because they were not to appear naked in the presence of God. Remember that God made clothing out of animal skins to cover the shame of Adam and Eve's sin. The same shame still hung over fallen man, which thereby necessitated that the priests not appear naked in any way in the presence of the Lord. The Israelites were never to be naked in the presence of God, as it revealed their sinfulness, guilt and shame. The priests were always to be clothed in their special garments.

The priest's garments in the light of the New Testament

When we cross over into the New Testament our minds should first of all dwell upon the identity of Christ as our high priest. Christ is our high priest but there is a great difference between his ministry and that of Aaron and his descendants. The author of Hebrews elaborates upon the differences between the priesthoods of Aaron and Christ: 'For every high priest chosen from among men is appointed to act on behalf of men in relation to God, to offer gifts and sacrifices for sins. He can deal gently with the ignorant and wayward, since he himself is beset with weakness. Because of this he is bound to offer sacrifice for his own sins just as he does for those of the people' (Heb. 5:1-3).

As we saw in the previous chapter, the high priest had to sacrifice a burnt offering so he could enter the presence of God in the holy of holies. Not only did the high priest have to sacrifice a bull for the sins of Israel, but also for his own sins. As the author of Hebrews states: 'he is bound to offer sacrifice for his own sins' (Heb. 5:3). Jesus Christ, as we know, was not only the high priest but also the sacrifice — the lamb without blemish. The apostle Peter powerfully writes: 'You were ransomed from the futile ways inherited from your forefathers, not with perishable things such as silver or gold, but with the precious blood of Christ, like that of a lamb without blemish or spot' (1 Peter 1:18-19).

So, then, one of the major differences between the Old Testament high priest and Christ as our high priest is the fact that the Levites were sinful and Christ was not. Not only did Christ not have to offer a sacrifice for himself because he is free from sin, but by the sacrifice of his own life he brings the actual forgiveness of sins: 'For if the sprinkling of defiled persons with the blood of goats and bulls and with the ashes of a heifer sanctifies for the purification of the flesh, how much more will the blood of Christ, who through the eternal Spirit offered himself without blemish to God, purify our conscience from dead works to serve the living God' (Heb. 9:13-14). So, then, we can rejoice knowing that by Christ's sacrifice on the cross, our sins accuse us no more. The slate, so to speak, which was filled with the record of our wrongs has been wiped clean; as far as the east is from the west, so God has removed our sins from us.

At the same time, we should realize that Christ does not merely wipe the slate clean and then tell us to fill it with our own righteousness. On the contrary, Christ not only wipes the slate clean, forgiving us from our sin, but he also gives us his perfect righteousness — the slate, if you will, is filled with the perfect, holy and righteous obedience of Jesus Christ. The accrediting or imputation of Christ's obedience to his people is attested in numerous places throughout the Scriptures. The prophet Isaiah writes: 'Out of the anguish of his soul he shall see and be satisfied; by his knowledge shall the righteous one, my servant, make many to be accounted righteous, and he shall bear their iniquities' (Isa. 53:11). Building upon this idea, Paul explains to the church in Rome: 'For as by the one man's disobedience the many were constituted sinners, so by the one man's obedience the many will be constituted righteous' (Rom. 5:19, translation mine). Or most famously, Paul writes of the glorious exchange that occurs between Christ and the believer: 'For our sake he made him to be sin who knew no sin, so that in him we might become the righteousness of God' (2 Cor. 5:21). So, then, when we place our faith in Christ, trusting in his life, death and resurrection, we not only receive the forgiveness of sins but also the imputation of Christ's righteousness. When God the Father then looks upon us he not only sees us negatively, namely, that we are without sin, but positively, that we are righteous in his sight.

Holiness and imputed righteousness were symbolically represented in the clothing of the high priest. Recall that God told Moses that the priest's garments were holy, 'for glory and for beauty' (Exod. 28:2). Moreover, the priests were not supposed to enter the presence of God with their nakedness exposed — that is, their sinfulness, guilt and shame. They were to have their sinfulness covered by their holy garments. It should come as no surprise, then, that the Scriptures liken the righteousness that we receive in salvation to being clothed in garments. The prophet Zechariah recounts a vision of Joshua the high priest who stood before the Lord in soiled filthy garments as Satan hurled accusations against the priest. Satan was rebuked by an angel and informed him that Joshua was a 'brand plucked from the fire', that is, delivered from God's wrath. The angel then told others to remove the priest's filthy garments. The removal of the garments is described as the removal of sin. Joshua is then clothed in pure garments, which implies that Joshua was now holy and righteous, free from sin (Zech. 3:1-5).

Elsewhere in the book of Isaiah, the garments of salvation are likened unto righteousness: 'I will greatly rejoice in the LORD; my soul shall exult in my God, for he has clothed me with the garments of salvation; he has covered me with the robe of righteousness, as a bridegroom decks himself like a priest with a beautiful headdress, and as a bride adorns herself with her jewels' (Isa. 61:10). It is important to note that the one who is saved does not manufacture his own garments; rather the garments are given by the Lord. The apostle John builds upon this Old Testament imagery when he writes: '"Let us rejoice and exult and give him the glory, for the marriage of the Lamb has come, and his Bride has made herself ready; it was granted her to clothe herself with fine linen, bright and pure" — for the fine linen is the righteous deeds of the saints' (Rev. 19:7-8). The saints are decked in a robe of righteousness, their righteous deeds, but these righteous deeds are given to the bride, not produced by the bride herself.

There is a theme of being clothed in righteousness, which we know we receive from our great high priest, Jesus Christ. We should rejoice in the knowledge that we are clothed in the perfect righteousness of Christ. We do not have to labour and somehow earn God's favour by our good works. Rather, when we place our faith in Christ, we receive the forgiveness of sins and the imputation of his righteousness. And these things are given to us by God's free and unmerited grace! Just as the garments of the high priest were for glory and beauty, in a far greater way we are clothed with Christ's robe of righteousness all to the glory and praise of our triune Lord.

There is one last thing we should take into consideration, namely, the breastpiece that Aaron wore. Recall that Aaron was wearing a replica of the tabernacle. It should come as no surprise that we see heaven itself foreshadowed in Aaron's breastpiece. Note that when the New Jerusalem descends out of the heavens in the book of Revelation, which is the church, it has the same features as Aaron's breastpiece:

> *Then came one of the seven angels who had the seven bowls full of the seven last plagues and spoke to me, saying, 'Come, I will show you the Bride, the wife of the Lamb.' And he carried me away in the Spirit to a great, high mountain, and showed me the holy city Jerusalem coming down out of heaven from God, having the glory of God, its radiance like a most rare jewel, like a jasper, clear as crystal*
>
> (Rev. 21:9-11).

The names of the twelve tribes of Israel are inscribed upon its twelve gates (Rev. 21:12). There are twelve foundations, with the names of the twelve apostles of Christ (Rev. 21:14). The city 'lies foursquare; its length the same as its width' (Rev. 21:16), just like the perfectly square breastpiece. And the foundation of the wall that surrounds the city is adorned with precious stones: jasper, sapphire, agate, emerald, onyx, carnelian, chrysolite, beryl, topaz, chrysoprase, jacinth and amethyst (Rev. 21:19-20). These are the same precious stones that adorned Aaron's breastpiece.

Conclusion

Aaron wore a miniature replica of the heavenly temple upon his chest and what we see hinted at in shadows will be fully revealed on the final day with the descent of the New Jerusalem, the holy temple, the church — radiant and resplendent with the righteousness of Christ! Rejoice that we no longer need to fear the presence of the Lord. We no longer need to sacrifice bulls and goats and worry whether we have the garments properly donned to avoid God's judgement. Instead, we have Jesus Christ the perfect, holy and righteous high priest who has offered himself as a sacrifice, bringing us the forgiveness of sins and giving us his own righteousness. Remember to rest in the perfect righteousness of Christ.

8
THE CONSECRATION OF THE PRIESTS

Read Exodus 29:1-46

Introduction

We return to the instructions for the construction of the tabernacle. We have explored the tabernacle and its furniture, and we last examined the clothing of the priests. This chapter explores the nature of the consecration, or the setting aside and dedication, of the priests for their service in the tabernacle. As we explore the consecration of the priests, one of the things that should strike us is the number of sacrifices that are necessary to purify ceremonially the priest for service. One thing that should strike us is the bloody nature of the priest's consecration. It tells us of the costly nature of sin and that, in the end, there is only one remedy available for one who is guilty of sin — the perfect sacrifice of Jesus Christ.

Explanation of the rite

Bringing the priests near (vv. 1-4)

The chapter opens with the instructions for bringing the priests near the tabernacle for their consecration. We should notice that before they entered the tent of meeting and before they donned their priestly garments, they were supposed to wash with water (v. 4). They were supposed to wash themselves from the bronze basin that stood before the tabernacle (Exod. 30:17-21). If the priests did not wash, then God would strike them down. They were also supposed to have the elements of the sacrificial animals, one bull and two rams, and the needed grain offerings ready as well.

Anointing the priests (vv. 5-9)

The priests were to dress themselves in their priestly garments and then they were to be anointed with oil, for which we see instructions in the next chapter (Exod. 30:22-33). The oil was to be used exclusively for the ordination and consecration of the priests. Anyone who used it for any other purpose would also be cut off from the people of God. There is also a specific purpose given for the anointing with oil, namely, it was to seal the permanence of the Aaronic priesthood: 'And the priesthood shall be theirs by a statute for ever. Thus you shall ordain Aaron and his sons' (Exod. 29:9).

The first sacrifice for the sins of the priests (vv. 10-14)

In these verses Aaron and his sons had to place their hands on the head of the bull, symbolizing the transfer of their sin to the bull. They then had to slaughter the bull, offer it as a burnt offering, and the rest of the bull — the head, skin and dung — they had to carry outside the camp for disposal. What is clear here is that the bull was a substitute for the priests — their sin was symbolically punished upon the altar as it was burned and cut off from the people of God by being taken outside the camp.

The second and third sacrificial animals (vv. 15-25)

Aaron and his sons were to lay their hands upon the second animal, a ram, and slaughter it, sprinkling its blood upon the sides of the

THE CONSECRATION OF THE PRIESTS

altar. They were then supposed to burn the entire ram upon the altar as a burnt offering to the Lord (v. 18). Aaron and his sons were then supposed to take a second animal, another ram, place their hands upon it, and then slaughter it. They were to take the blood of this second ram and sprinkle it, along with the anointing oil, upon Aaron and his garments, as well as those of his sons. This action was to dedicate the priests, make them holy, and purify them from sin. They were also supposed to take the blood of this ram and put some of it on Aaron's right ear lobe, on his right thumb, and on the big toe of his right foot. This was also to be done to Aaron's sons. The remainder of the blood was to be sprinkled upon the side of the altar. Now, the precise reason for placing the blood upon the right ear lobe, thumb and big toe, is not revealed in the text. We do know, however, that the general purpose of this practice was to ceremonially cleanse the priest from his sin. The priests were supposed to take the various cakes of grain and figs, raise them before the Lord, and then offer them upon the altar as a burnt offering.

The priestly consumption of meat (vv. 26-34)

Aaron and his sons were to take some of the meat that was left from the second ram, the breast, and this was their portion that they were allowed to eat. Any of the meat or bread that was left over was to be burned. Again, no one was allowed to eat this food — it was for the priests alone: 'They shall eat those things with which atonement was made at their ordination and consecration, but an outsider shall not eat of them, because they are holy' (Exod. 29:33).

The daily priestly offerings (vv. 35-37)

Aaron and his sons were consecrated over a seven-day period, which seems to reflect the initial creation of man, who was also the first priest. We should note, though, that Aaron and his sons had to sacrifice a bull on each of the seven days. So, at this point, there were seven bulls and two rams that were required for the consecration of the priests. These sacrifices were not the only required sacrifices. Remember, the sacrifices of the seven bulls and two rams were required for the priests alone, there were also the sins of the people that had to be taken into account.

The daily sacrifices (vv. 38-44)

In addition for the priestly sacrifices, God also instructed the priests to make two daily sacrifices on behalf of the people. These sacrifices were performed at the beginning and end of the day — morning and evening. Two lambs were to be offered for these sacrifices, one at the morning and the other in the evening. Again, these sacrifices were for the ceremonial cleansing of the people from their sins. To what end were all of these sacrifices not only for Aaron and the people? We read: 'It shall be a regular burnt offering throughout your generations at the entrance of the tent of meeting before the LORD, where I will meet with you, to speak to you there. There I will meet with the people of Israel, and it shall be sanctified by my glory ... I will dwell among the people of Israel and will be their God' (Exod. 29:42-45). The ultimate purpose of all of these sacrifices was so that the people of God could have the presence and fellowship of God in their midst. But because of the entrance of sin, fellowship with God came at a high price — as we see that much blood had to be shed in order to maintain their relationship with their covenant Lord.

The consecration in the light of the New Testament

The perfect sacrifice of Christ

What we have seen in the instructions for the consecration of the priests and the institution of daily sacrifices was the establishment

THE CONSECRATION OF THE PRIESTS

of a sacrificial system. We know, however, that this sacrificial system was only a shadow of the ultimate sacrifice that would be instituted by Christ himself. Indeed, God instituted a system of sacrifices to be carried out by the anointed priests. Well, the anointed, the Messiah, has instituted a new sacrificial order. The author of Hebrews tells us: 'For since the law has but a shadow of the good things to come instead of the true form of these realities, it can never, by the same sacrifices that are continually offered every year, make perfect those who draw near' (Heb. 10:1). The author also writes: 'For it is impossible for the blood of bulls and goats to take away sins' (Heb. 10:4).

By contrast, Christ's perfect sacrifice was of an entirely different order. The author of Hebrews writes that Christ abolished the first order to establish the second (Heb. 10:9). The sacrifices of the bulls and rams, or goats, only pointed to the all-sufficient sacrifice of Jesus Christ. With the once-and-for-all sacrifice of Christ, we as the people of God no longer have to repeatedly offer sacrifices so that we can be in the presence of God.

On the contrary, Christ has offered himself once and for all, putting away the need for sacrifice because he has paid the debt that we owe for our sins: 'And by that will we have been sanctified through the offering of the body of Jesus Christ once for all. And every priest stands daily at his service, offering repeatedly the same sacrifices, which can never take away sins' (Heb. 10:10-11). Indeed, the sacrifices of the Aaronic priests were necessary because they themselves were constantly guilty of sin. They had to sacrifice seven bulls and two rams for their own consecration and then two sacrifices per day for the sins of the people. Yet because Christ was sinless, he was the spotless lamb who was slain, he had no need for his own sacrifice. Rather, his sacrifice was an outpouring of his love and mercy upon those who did not deserve such love.

CHRIST AND THE DESERT TABERNACLE

How then should we live?

In light of the all-sufficient once-for-all sacrifice of Christ, the author of Hebrews instructs his recipients to do three things. First, we read:

> *Therefore, brothers, since we have confidence to enter the holy places by the blood of Jesus, by the new and living way that he opened for us through the curtain, that is, through his flesh, and since we have a great priest over the house of God, let us draw near with a true heart in full assurance of faith, with our hearts sprinkled clean from an evil conscience and our bodies washed with pure water*
>
> (Heb. 10:19-22).

The author tells us that we should draw near to God with a true heart in full assurance of faith. The Old Testament priests had much to fear as they drew near to God — perhaps in a moment of absentmindedness a priest might forget to perform one of the rituals in the proper manner. For such an oversight, the penalty was death. Yet, we need not fear such things because Christ has offered the once-for-all perfect sacrifice on our behalf.

We should therefore constantly draw near to the presence of God — whether through prayer, the reading of the Word, or corporate worship. Remember that the purpose of the sacrifices was so that the people could be in the presence of God and fellowship with him. But remember, too, that the sacrificial price was very high. The sacrifice on our behalf was very costly — the Father sacrificed his only Son for us so that we could be reconciled to him. Should we therefore not draw near to God through the appointed means, fellowship, and be in the presence of our faithful covenant Lord?

The author of Hebrews gives a second instruction: 'Let us hold fast the confession of our hope without wavering, for he who promised

THE CONSECRATION OF THE PRIESTS

is faithful' (Heb. 10:23). We should never lose hope no matter what trials or tribulations we face. Whether we face personal illness, persecution, financial difficulties, problems at work, problems at school — no matter what trial we suffer, we should never lose sight of the source of our hope. Jesus Christ has brought us what no one could — fellowship with our Creator and Maker.

Think of the thousands of years that God's people longed for intimate fellowship with our covenant Lord — think of the sacrifices that Abel, Adam and Eve, and the faithful offered, longing and looking forward to the time when complete fellowship would be restored to them by the seed of the woman. Well, God has been faithful to send his Son to fulfil the promises that he has made. God is faithful; we should therefore never lose hope.

The author of Hebrews gives a third instruction: 'And let us consider how to stir up one another to love and good works, not neglecting to meet together, as is the habit of some, but encouraging one another, and all the more as you see the Day drawing near' (Heb. 10:24-25). Notice that as a result of the once-for-all sacrifice of Christ, we are to stir up one another to love and good works. We should be in prayer for one another that we would all be more and more conformed to the image of Christ. We should stir up one another to love and good works, not so much by what we say, but by our lives.

We can stir one another up to these things by loving others and performing good works for others — not so we can swell with pride or somehow try to merit God's favour, but in response to the once-for-all sacrifice of Christ. We can also pray for one another that we as the church would love Christ, one another, and do good works to the glory of Christ. How often, for example, do we pray for those who we know are sinning? Do we pray for those under church discipline? Do we encourage those under discipline to love Christ, his body, and to glorify Christ by their lives?

The chief way that the author of Hebrews has in mind to accomplish the goal of stirring up one another to love and good works is through attending church. He tells his readers, not to neglect 'to meet together, as is the habit of some, but encouraging one another' (v. 25). In other words, if we truly have a longing to be in the presence of God, and we realize how costly a price has been paid so that we have free access to our covenant Lord, then we will hardly ever miss a worship service because our desire will be to be in his presence.

Conclusion

As we reflect upon the consecration of the priests, we should not be revolted by the number of animal sacrifices that had to be performed. We should not be repulsed by the amount of blood that had to be shed. We should not be disgusted by the slaughter of animals so that the people of God could be in the presence of our Lord. We should instead be ashamed of our sinfulness that has required such sacrifices.

We should, however, rejoice that we have a merciful God who opened the way to reconciliation by showing us in shadows the costly nature of the sacrifice of his only Son. We should realize that the sacrifice of Christ is not only our forgiveness of sins but indeed our sustenance for life itself. Remember that the priests were allowed to eat a portion of the sacrifices from the altar for their food. We are a holy nation of priests, and God has allowed us to eat from the altar of sacrifice: 'Do not be led away by diverse and strange teachings, for it is good for the heart to be strengthened by grace, not by foods, which have not benefited those devoted to them. We have an altar from which those who serve the tent have no right to eat' (Heb. 13:9-10). We are sustained by the sacrifice of Christ. Therefore draw near to our Lord! Be filled with hope! Stir one another up to love and good works! And do not neglect gathering together as we wait until the day of our Lord's return.

9

THE ALTAR OF INCENSE

Read Exodus 30:1-10 (37:25-28)

Introduction

We have seen various pieces of furniture of the tabernacle, the ark, the lampstand, the table for the showbread, the altar for burnt offerings, and the outer courtyard. We have also explored various aspects of the priest and his responsibilities, whether his garments or the ritual for his ordination and consecration. Now we return to the entrance of the holy of holies, and this time it is to examine the altar of incense. While there is not much within the immediate context to suggest the function and purpose of the altar of incense, there is a greater amount of information found in other parts of Scripture.

It is good for us to remember that the earthly tabernacle is a copy of the heavenly temple. Recall what the author of Hebrews tells us regarding the earthly tabernacle: 'They serve a copy and shadow of the heavenly things. For when Moses was about to erect the tent, he was instructed by God, saying, "See that you make everything according to the pattern that was shown you on the mountain"' (Heb. 8:5). So, this chapter will explore the altar within its immediate context and then see what the New Testament has to say about its significance.

Indeed, what the New Testament tells us is that the altar of incense was supposed ultimately to represent the prayers of God's people constantly arising before his presence. Let us see how this is so and learn the importance of prayer, as it is a vital part of the tabernacle as well as the final dwelling place of God, the last temple, the church. For in doing this, we will see not only how the altar of incense is connected to our high priest, Jesus Christ, but also to us, the church.

The features of the altar

The beginning of the chapter tells us that the Israelites were supposed to construct the altar of incense out of acacia wood, like the rest of the furnishings in the tabernacle. It was supposed to be about 1.5 feet long and 1.5 feet wide, in other words, a perfect cube. And, it was supposed to be three feet tall. They were to overlay the altar with gold. The altar was supposed to have gold rings and poles, so that it would be mobile and carried about like the rest of the tabernacle furnishings — such as the ark and the table for the bread of presence. The altar was to stand in front of the veil that separated the holy of holies from the rest of the inner tabernacle.

This altar, as its title tells us, was supposed to be for the burning of incense, not for any other type of sacrifice, such as animals or grain offerings: 'You shall not offer unauthorized incense on it, or a burnt offering, or a grain offering, and you shall not pour a drink offering on it' (Exod. 30:9). Moreover, verse 7 tells us that it was supposed to be 'fragrant' incense. Scholars surmise that one of the purposes of the fragrant incense was to cover the other malodorous smells that would have been in the air, such as those generated by the animal sacrifices. Cooking might have a pleasant aroma, but

THE ALTAR OF INCENSE

when an animal is gutted, other less pleasant smells are produced, particularly when an animal is disembowelled.

Aaron was supposed to burn incense on the altar both in the morning and evening, when he dressed the lamps. Once a year he was to take the blood of a sacrificial animal and ceremonially cleanse the altar. Again, the idea is that everything in the tabernacle needed to be ceremonially purified from the contamination of sin, because sinful human beings were constantly in contact with the furnishings of the tabernacle.

Here in the immediate context we do not get much more information regarding the purpose of the altar of incense, except for the implicit information that the incense was obviously supposed to release a fragrant aroma throughout the tabernacle. We find further information, however, regarding the purpose of the altar from Leviticus: 'And he shall take a censer full of coals of fire from the altar before the LORD, and two handfuls of sweet incense beaten small, and he shall bring it inside the veil and put the incense on the fire before the LORD, that the cloud of the incense may cover the mercy seat that is over the testimony, so that he does not die' (Lev. 16:12-13). On the Day of Atonement, the high priest was to burn incense on the altar and bring some of the incense in the censer into the holy of holies; the cloud of smoke that was supposed to arise from the censer would cover the Ark of the Covenant. The cloud would cover the Ark and place a barrier between the high priest and the presence of the Lord, which would prevent the high priest from being struck dead.

So, then, the smoke from the altar of incense was a layer of protection for the high priest. Now from the Old Testament we do not receive much more information regarding the altar of incense. The New Testament, however, does shed more light upon its function and purpose.

CHRIST AND THE DESERT TABERNACLE

The altar in the light of the New Testament

When the apostle John was drawn up to heaven in his revelatory vision, he beheld the heavenly temple, the pattern upon which the earthly temple was built. John observed the worship of the lamb and the use of golden bowls of incense. The burning incense, John tells us, were the prayers of the saints (Rev. 5:8). We find another passage from Revelation that further elaborates upon the nature of the incense in the heavenly temple: 'And another angel came and stood at the altar with a golden censer, and he was given much incense to offer with the prayers of all the saints on the golden altar before the throne, and the smoke of the incense, with the prayers of the saints, rose before God from the hand of the angel' (Rev. 8:3-4). These two passages provide us with some guidance regarding the altar of incense.

Remember that the heavenly temple is definitive for the earthly tabernacle, the shadow or copy of the heavenly. So, then, it appears that the altar of incense was to be a reminder to the high priest of the need for prayer in the presence of the Lord. The prayers of the high priest were supposed to rise with the smoke from the altar, just as we see in the imagery from Revelation — smoke and prayers mingled together. This means that the altar of incense should draw our attention to the prayers of the high priest, and also the prayers of God's people. Let us first consider the prayers of the high priest.

The prayers of our high priest

I believe that one of the elements of the work of Christ of which many within the church are unfamiliar are the intercessory prayers that Christ offered up for his people, the church. Christ's high priestly prayer appears in the seventeenth chapter of John's Gospel. Notice for whom Christ specifically prays: 'For I have given them the words that you gave me, and they have received them and

THE ALTAR OF INCENSE

have come to know in truth that I came from you; and they have believed that you sent me. I am praying for them. I am not praying for the world but for those whom you have given me, for they are yours' (John 17:8-9). Christ prays specifically for the church; in other words, the prayer we find in John 17 is specifically for us individually as we are united together as the body of Christ. Like the prayers of the high priest in the tabernacle, Christ's prayers ascended like the smoke of incense as a pleasing aroma to his heavenly Father. On our behalf, Christ specifically prayed for us, but what specifically did Christ ask of his Father?

Christ first prayed that we would be filled with joy: 'I am coming to you, and these things I speak in the world, that they may have my joy fulfilled in themselves' (John 17:13). Christ also prayed that we would be protected from the evil one, from Satan: 'I do not ask that you take them out of the world, but that you keep them from the evil one' (John 17.15). Christ could have prayed that in the face of the evil in the world the Father would have taken us out of the world. If we were taken out of the world, then we would not be able to testify to the truth of the gospel, to the person and work of Christ. In effect, there would be no light in the dark world. So, since withdrawal from the world is not an option, Christ prayed that the Father would protect us from the evil one, from Satan himself.

Christ also prayed for our sanctification and growth in the knowledge of the word: 'Sanctify them in the truth; your word is truth' (John 17:17). That we understand the Scriptures and that they are profitable for our sanctification is the direct result of Christ's prayer on our behalf. In addition to these petitions, we also see that Christ prayed for our unity with our triune Lord, which has some consequences, glory and unity:

> *I do not ask for these only, but also for those who will believe in me through their word, that they may all be one, just as*

you, Father, are in me, and I in you, that they also may be in us, so that the world may believe that you have sent me. The glory that you have given me I have given to them, that they may be one even as we are one, I in them and you in me, that they may become perfectly one, so that the world may know that you sent me and loved them even as you loved me

(John 17:20-23).

Perhaps we do not realize it, but our very existence and growth in grace, our sanctification and strength flows not only from the power of the Holy Spirit but also from the intercessory prayer of Christ, our great high priest.

At the same time, however, we should realize that Christ's priestly intercession did not finish with his earthly ministry. On the contrary, we read in the book of Hebrews: 'Consequently, he is able to save to the uttermost those who draw near to God through him, since he always lives to make intercession for them' (Heb. 7:25). In other words, at this very moment, Christ is in the heavenly holy of holies making intercession for us. Yes, Christ offered his once-for-all sacrifice on our behalf and his sacrificial work on our behalf is finished. Indeed, Christ completed his sacrificial work when he cried out: 'It is finished,' upon the cross. But Christ continues to intercede for his people, for those who draw near to God through him, as the author to the Hebrews tells us.

The prayers of the priests

How is it that we draw near to God but through prayer? We must not forget that while Christ is our high priest, we too are priests. The apostle Peter tells the church: 'But you are a chosen race, a royal priesthood, a holy nation, a people for his own possession, that you may proclaim the excellencies of him who called you out of darkness into his marvellous light' (1 Peter 2:9). We are priests

THE ALTAR OF INCENSE

who serve God in his final dwelling place, the final temple, the church. Though we do not serve a physical building, in the sense of brick and mortar, that does not mean we should not offer up incense.

When I write that we should offer up incense, I do not mean that we should break out the incense ball and that our worship should be marked by smells and bells, like the worship of Roman Catholicism. Rather, we should continually offer up the incense of prayer, that our prayers, like the smoke of incense, would rise to the heavens just as it would for the priests serving in the tabernacle. This means that we should pray on all sorts of occasions and for all sorts of things. We should, of course, pray during worship, when the temple, the people of God, is gathered together as a body. In such circumstances, we should pray with one another, and with the minister when he offers up prayers on behalf of the congregation. We should not only pray *with* the minister but *for* him, that the Lord would use him in the ministry of word and sacraments.

We should not limit our prayers, however, to gathered worship but offer them at any and all times. Paul wrote to the church at Ephesus that they should pray at all times in the Spirit with all prayer and supplication so that they would persevere and intercede on behalf of the saints, the church (Eph. 6:18). Remember, there is no need that is too small, as God has even the hairs of our heads numbered. Christ tells us: 'And do not fear those who kill the body but cannot kill the soul. Rather fear him who can destroy both soul and body in hell. Are not two sparrows sold for a penny? And not one of them will fall to the ground apart from your Father. But even the hairs of your head are all numbered. Fear not, therefore; you are of more value than many sparrows' (Matt. 10:28-31). This means that we can take our needs and desires to our heavenly Father. It also means that we should intercede on behalf of others within the body of Christ, the church.

There are certainly many needs that the people of God have. Not only should we pray for the people of God, but we should pray for all sorts of people. Paul counselled Timothy, a young pastor, to pray for all people, including kings and those in positions of authority (1 Tim. 2:1-2). But Paul's advice was not restricted to Timothy alone. What is good for the goose, the pastor, is also good for the gander, the church! We should therefore pray for political leaders, even those with whom we might disagree. The prayers we offer on behalf of our political leaders should not be based upon whether we agree or disagree with the policies they enact. We should also pray for unbelievers, that they would see their need for Christ, repent, and place their faith in Christ.

Something from which we all suffer, is that we often doubt the power of prayer. I think the reason we doubt the power of prayer is not because it is powerless but because we do not take our needs to God in prayer. When we fail to do so, we fail to see the power of prayer. If we do not ask, we do not receive. If we desire to bolster the exercise of faith in prayer, we should flee to the words of Christ and pray that he would increase our faith and devotion to prayer: 'Truly, I say to you, if you have faith and do not doubt, you will not only do what has been done to the fig tree, but even if you say to this mountain, "Be taken up and thrown into the sea," it will happen. And whatever you ask in prayer, you will receive, if you have faith' (Matt. 21:21-22).

Conclusion

When we contemplate the altar of incense, our minds should ultimately be drawn to the subject of prayer. Our minds should first fall upon the priestly prayers of our own high priest, Jesus Christ, on our behalf; and not only his priestly intercession for us while he was here on the earth but also his intercession for us even now at this very moment in the heavenly holy of holies. Our minds

THE ALTAR OF INCENSE

should also drift to our own prayer life. The priests were supposed to offer incense in the morning and evening.

Perhaps this is instructive for our own prayers — that we should offer prayers morning and evening, prayers of thanksgiving, praise and adoration for the work of Jesus Christ our high priest. We should offer up prayers of intercession on behalf of the people of God, for their needs and for their sanctification. We should offer up prayers of intercession for those in the world, regardless of whether they are in high or low positions. In the end, it should be our prayer that our prayers would ascend like the incense in the tabernacle and would be a pleasing aroma to our great and faithful covenant Lord.

10

THE CENSUS TAX

Read Exodus 30:11-16

Introduction

What we find in the text before us is the instruction for taking a census tax. Now, taking a census tax might seem like a rather perfunctory task. In the United States a census is taken every ten years, and anyone with a job knows the responsibility and obligation of paying taxes. This census and tax, however, are of an entirely different nature. Recalling Israel's history, taking a census was a very dangerous thing. King David brought God's judgement upon Israel for his unauthorized census of the nation to determine the size of his army. But on the other hand, we also can see from this text that collecting the tax is essentially atonement money. In other words, this census tax is somehow connected to the forgiveness of sins. But far from being a crass exchange of money for salvation, let us see why God has Israel take a census and in what way the collected money serves as atonement money. As we can well imagine, the ultimate significance of these instructions finds its resting place in Christ and therefore also connects to us, the church, his body.

The census tax

We read the following instructions regarding the census and tax:

> *When you take the census of the people of Israel, then each shall give a ransom for his life to the* LORD *when you number them, that there be no plague among them when you number them. Each one who is numbered in the census shall give this: half a shekel according to the shekel of the sanctuary (the shekel is twenty gerahs), half a shekel as an offering to the* LORD
> (Exod. 30:12-13).

Notice that Israel was expected to take a census, or count the number of Israelites in the nation, from time to time. Israel was commanded to take a census, for example, before they entered the promised land so they could find out how many soldiers they had. Yet, at the same time, if they only took a census by itself, it would result in a plague.

We know of the consequences of an unauthorized census when King David took a census against the advice of his chief general, Joab: 'But Joab said to the king, "May the LORD your God add to the people a hundred times as many as they are, while the eyes of my lord the king still see it, but why does my lord the king delight in this thing"' (2 Sam. 24:3)? It seems that Joab saw the danger in David's order for a census — he was fearful because David was 'counting his chickens', so to speak, and was looking for confidence in the number of soldiers he had rather than seeking his strength in the Lord.

Even though Joab counted some 1.3 million fighting men (2 Sam. 24:9), we know from other examples that it was the Lord who defeated Israel's enemies. Two striking examples of this arose when God had Israel defeat the city of Jericho by commanding Israel to march around it seven times. God also defeated Israel's enemies when he whittled Gideon's army from 22,000 to 300 men (Judg. 7). For David's sinful census Israel endured three days of plague, which claimed the lives of 70,000 men (2 Sam. 24:15).

To prevent a plague from falling upon Israel when they took the census, each man was to give a ransom, or literally an *atonement*, for his life. This atonement payment amounted to half a shekel, which is about 5.7 grams of silver, or about the equivalent weight of eight small pieces of candy. Anyone who was numbered in the census twenty years or older, rich or poor, was to give their half-shekel offering to the tabernacle, and make atonement for their lives.

Notice what purpose the atonement money was to serve: 'You shall take the atonement money from the people of Israel and shall give it for the service of the tent of meeting, that it may bring the people of Israel to remembrance before the Lord, so as to make atonement for your lives' (Exod. 30:16). The Israelites were not simply trading money for their salvation. That charge has certainly been levelled at the church over the years, whether by the likes of Karl Marx, who said that religion was the opiate of the masses, or Frederick Nietzsche, who argued that the church invented the idea of sin so it could take money from the ignorant masses and keep them under the church's thumb. And, unfortunately, the church has slipped into such sinful practices.

It was the sale of indulgences by the Roman Catholic Church during the sixteenth century which sparked the Reformation. Originally, the church needed money to construct St Peter's cathedral in Rome. Anyone who gave money to the church was granted an indulgence, a partial or full pardon from time in purgatory — a 'thank you' for the donation. By the time the practice made it to the common man on the street, the slogan rang out: 'As soon as the coin in the coffer rings, the soul from purgatory springs.'

Here in our text, however, the atonement money was neither an invention to keep people in check, nor a crass exchange of money for forgiveness. Instead, notice that the offering was to bring 'Israel to remembrance before the Lord' (v. 16). In other words, the atonement money functioned in the same way as the dedication of the firstborn of Israel. When Israel first celebrated the Passover, God struck down the firstborn of Egypt in judgement. But the firstborn of Israel were spared, not because of their superiority over the Egyptians but because they were under the blood of the Passover lamb. God therefore had the Israelites dedicate all of their firstborn, both man and animal, to the Lord as a reminder of their redemption.

In other words, when the Israelites took a census, the natural inclination would be to take pride in their great numbers, forgetting that they were redeemed from the bonds of slavery in Egypt by their covenant Lord. This was David's sin in taking the census, and is why the plague fell upon Israel. Yet, if the Israelites took a census, they were also to collect the tax and give it to the tabernacle as a multifaceted reminder of their redemption. The census tax was a reminder that God had redeemed them from Egypt. The tax was also given to the tabernacle, again, as a reminder of Israel's sinfulness and need for the intercessory work of the high priest and sacrificial system so they could be in God's presence.

The census tax in the light of the New Testament

As we cross over to the New Testament and consider this practice in the light of Christ, we should first realize that there is no direct connection to a corresponding New Testament practice. For example, we see various connections between the Passover and the Lord's Supper, or the sacrifices of the tabernacle and Christ, or the Red Sea crossing and baptism. But the census tax, while having no direct corresponding New Testament practice, still has significance in the light of Christ and therefore a connection to us, the church.

THE CENSUS TAX

The connection between the census tax and the New Testament church lies ultimately with Christ's relationship to the tabernacle. The tabernacle in its architecture and sacrifices pointed to Christ, the fulfilment of these shadows and types. We have certainly seen these connections over the last several chapters. Keeping the connection between Christ and the church in mind, then, we should recognize that the census tax was a reminder to the Israelites that they were redeemed by their covenant Lord — they were bought at a price. The census tax was a reminder to the Israelites not to consider themselves too important or somehow worthy of their redemption. In other words, it was a reminder to keep their pride and arrogance in check. The census tax was supposed to turn Israel's attention to their redemption. Well, we certainly see these same reminders throughout the New Testament in light of Christ's costly sacrifice on our behalf. There are several areas where we find the principle of the census tax at work in connection with the sacrifice of Christ.

We are not worthy of our redemption

Sometimes when we take a census of our lives, if I can put it in those terms, pride can easily swell in our hearts. We look at our morality, and compare it with the morality of the world. We generally do not lie, cheat, or steal. We hold respectable jobs, have respectable children who make decent grades, and we believe we offer a positive contribution to society as a whole. When we see criminals on the TV news, or hear of crimes such as murder, rape and theft, we think we are above such sins.

This is especially a problem for Christians who work in law enforcement, for example. The tendency might easily be one of, 'I'm better than the people who I arrest.' Christ told a parable that well explains this mindset. He spoke of two men who went to the temple to pray, a 'godly' Pharisee and a despised tax collector.

The 'godly' Pharisee took a census of his life and thanked God that he was not like extortionists, the unjust, adulterers, or like the despised tax collector beside him at the temple. The Pharisee thought to himself, 'I fast twice a week; I give tithes of all that I get.' The despised tax collector, on the other hand, did not want to draw nearer than he was and would not lift his head to look to heaven. Instead, he pounded his chest with his fist and begged the Lord, 'God, be merciful to me, a sinner!' Of these two men, Jesus tells us that the despised tax collector, not the 'godly' Pharisee went home justified, that is, declared righteous in God's sight (Luke 18:10-14). The tax collector did not want to take a census, or an inventory, of his life because he knew that only God's grace would save him, not his own sinful efforts.

The census tax reminded the Israelites that it was not their strength or moral rectitude that separated them from the rest of the nations, but rather the mercy and grace of God, which had been given to them through the promise of redemption through the work of the Messiah. God was kind to show his grace to a small, helpless, feeble, stiff-necked people — he redeemed them out of bondage because of his grace, and nothing else.

The same may be said about us — we have not been redeemed because of our strength, wealth, or moral righteousness, but because God showed us mercy in Christ. Paul rebuked the Corinthians because they continually took an inventory of their lives and believed that they were superior over one another. Paul pointedly asked the Corinthians: 'For who sees anything different in you? What do you have that you did not receive? If then you received it, why do you boast as if you did not receive it?' (1 Cor. 4:7). Paul reminded the Corinthians that they had not been chosen because of their superiority over others, but because of their inferiority! Paul writes:

THE CENSUS TAX

> *But God chose what is foolish in the world to shame the wise; God chose what is weak in the world to shame the strong; God chose what is low and despised in the world, even things that are not, to bring to nothing things that are, so that no human being might boast in the presence of God. He is the source of your life in Christ Jesus, whom God made our wisdom and our righteousness and sanctification and redemption. Therefore, as it is written, 'Let the one who boasts, boast in the Lord'* (1 Cor. 1:27-31).

Israel, therefore, was supposed to boast in the redemption of their covenant Lord, not their own pretended strength. Likewise we must constantly be reminded, as we gather for worship, that we cannot boast in ourselves when we take a census, or inventory, of our lives. Rather, everything we have is due to God's grace in Christ. Our boast should constantly be in the Lord and what he has done for us in Christ.

A reminder of our sinfulness and need for redemption

Something else the census tax was supposed to remind the Israelites of was their sinfulness and their need for redemption. Their census tax was an atonement for their lives — in other words, sin and death had a claim upon them, yet God had delivered and redeemed them, but at a price. The cost of their redemption was foreshadowed in the sacrifice of the Passover lamb, the required sacrifices of the tabernacle, and even the census tax.

We certainly know of the costly sacrifice for our redemption — the sacrifice of Jesus Christ. The apostle Peter tells us: '…you were ransomed from the futile ways inherited from your forefathers, not with perishable things such as silver or gold, but with the precious blood of Christ, like that of a lamb without blemish or spot' (1 Peter 1:18-19). So as we gather in worship each and every Lord's Day, we are reminded, among many other things, of the costly price of our redemption.

One of the things we have certainly seen throughout this survey of the tabernacle is the costly nature of the sacrifices. Many animals were slaughtered to remind the Israelites of their sin and the costly nature of their redemption. This is something that we perhaps are not able to appreciate as readily, most likely because the sacrifice of Christ is at some historical distance from us.

We need to think of the sacrifice in the following terms. A seminary professor of mine once wanted to impress upon his students the nature of a substitutionary atonement. He announced to his class that everyone in the class would receive an 'A' grade regardless of the quality of their work. Naturally, the students were surprised and excited at the prospects of an easy mark. But then the professor made a stipulation. In order for the class to receive an 'A', one person had to come forward and voluntarily receive an 'F' on behalf of the class. At first the students thought the professor was joking; but he was not. He told the class they would have a day to find a volunteer, otherwise they would all receive an 'F'. A student eventually came forward and volunteered to receive an 'F' on behalf of her classmates. The professor was despised, but I suspect that the whole class understood in a new way the costly nature of a substitutionary sacrifice.

Few if any would want to make such a sacrifice for others, let alone the sacrifice of giving one's own Son to die in the place of those who are worthy of condemnation. Who of us would be willing to sacrifice one of our children so that a murderer, rapist, or thief could be released from prison and have his criminal record erased for ever? This is just a hint of the nature of the Father's and Son's costly sacrifice on our behalf. Paul writes: 'For while we were still weak, at the right time Christ died for the ungodly. For one will scarcely die for a righteous person — though perhaps for a good person one would dare even to die — but God shows his love for us in that while we were still sinners, Christ died for us' (Rom. 5:6-8).

If this is the costly nature of our sacrifice, then, we should constantly meditate upon the price that has been paid, which informs our conduct. Again Paul writes: 'Flee from sexual immorality. Every other sin a person commits is outside the body, but the sexually immoral person sins against his own body. Or do you not know that your body is a temple of the Holy Spirit within you, whom you have from God? You are not your own, for you were bought with a price. So glorify God in your body' (1 Cor. 6:18-20). We have been freed from the bondage of Satan, sin and death, and have been crucified and raised with Christ to walk in the newness of life. If we truly appreciate the costly price of our redemption, the costly atonement that Christ has offered on our behalf, then we will not use the grace of God as a pretence or licence for sin. On the contrary: 'Let not sin therefore reign in your mortal bodies, to make you obey their passions. Do not present your members to sin as instruments for unrighteousness, but present yourselves to God as those who have been brought from death to life, and your members to God as instruments for righteousness' (Rom. 6:12-13).

Conclusion

We should meditate upon the passage before us and consider that Israel was supposed to be reminded of several things with the census tax. First, they were to be reminded that their strength came not from themselves but from the Lord. In other words, the census tax was to instil humility in them. Second, they were to be drawn to the tabernacle, which was a reminder of their sinfulness and need for redemption.

While we have no census tax, each and every Lord's Day as we gather for worship we should be reminded of the very same realities. We should be reminded that we of all people should be the most humble — we are not worthy of our redemption but recipients of God's favour and grace in Christ. When we look at unbelievers and their gross sins, we should never think that we are better than they, but instead remember that we would be just as lost and under God's wrath were it not for the grace of God in Christ.

And, we should also be reminded of the costly nature of our redemption — that God sent his only begotten Son to die on our behalf and that God's grace is therefore not a licence to sin. Rather, our desire should be, as Paul exhorted the church in Rome, to use our bodies as instruments for righteousness.

11

THE BRONZE BASIN

Read Exodus 30:17-21 (38:8)

Introduction

From a cursory reading of this passage, we can easily ascertain that the priests used the basin for washing their hands and feet. The basin, however, is not simply for washing off dirt. The basin was supposed to rest in the courtyard of the temple, which is a shadow and copy of the heavenly temple. That the basin is a copy of elements of the heavenly temple informs us there is far greater significance to this basin filled with water — it is no mere wash bowl! Ultimately, this chapter will show that the basin is connected to the waters of baptism and the person and work of the Holy Spirit. This baptism-Spirit connection also means that the basin, like all of the other elements of the tabernacle, is connected to the person and work of Christ, and also therefore to us, the church.

The bronze basin

Immediate context

When we read the Lord's instructions to Moses, the text states that the Israelites were supposed to construct a basin made out of bronze, and they were to fill the basin with water. The basin was supposed to sit between the altar and the tabernacle — that is, upon entering the compound, one would first see the altar for burnt offerings, then the bronze basin, and then the tent of meeting. The general idea seems to be that the priest would first offer the sacrifice of burnt offering which, as we can all imagine, would involve getting bloody. The priest would therefore proceed to the bronze basin and wash his hands and feet to remove the sacrificial blood. The bronze basin and its requisite washings, however, were not just for washing the hands and feet of blood or dirt.

The Lord is clear: if they did not wash their hands and feet, whether before they offered the sacrifice, after, or before entering the tent of meeting, they would die. In other words, the bronze altar was not just for removing blood but was tied to the symbolic cleansing of sin. Keeping in mind this connection with the cleansing from sin, we should take a step back and examine the broader picture from the rest of Scripture.

The heavenly temple and the Flood

As we take a step back, recall that the tabernacle is a shadow or copy of the heavenly temple. If this is the case, then we have an idea as to why there is a washbasin with water beside the tabernacle: there is a body of water beside the throne of God in the heavenly temple. The apostle John saw a great sea of glass beside the throne of God in his vision of the heavenly temple (Rev. 4:6). So, then, the basin is a copy of the sea of glass before the throne of God.

With this connection between the earthly and heavenly temple in mind, we remind ourselves of the opening verses of the Bible. Genesis tells us that the earth was covered in water but that God placed an expanse between the waters above and the waters below. It is important to note that God calls the expanse *heaven* (Gen. 1:6-8). In a word, the expanse is neither the sky nor the clouds in the sky, but rather the floor of the invisible heavens itself. The expanse separates the waters that lie before the throne of God from the waters on the earth below.

After the Fall, when the earth became filled with wickedness, God determined that he was going to judge the earth by the Flood. Many are under the impression that God simply caused it to rain really hard for forty days, and this profound amount of precipitation caused the Flood. A careful reading of the Genesis narrative, however, tells us that the Flood was not only a natural event, that is, it rained really hard, but it was also a supernatural event. God both caused the fountains of the deep to release great amounts of water, and also opened the 'windows of the heavens' (Gen. 7:11-12). In other words, God unleashed the heavenly sea of glass upon the earth in judgement against sin. In judgement, God took the creation and returned it to the conditions of Genesis 1:2 when the earth was without form and void, and darkness was over the face of the deep. Through the outpouring of the heavenly basin, if you will, God cleansed the creation of its wickedness by using water, not only the water of the lower creation, but especially the water that sat before his throne.

It also should not surprise us to see the use of water in cleansing the creation but also the accompanying work of the Holy Spirit. The apostle Peter informs us that the waters of the Flood are connected to the waters of baptism:

> ...once the Divine longsuffering waited in the days of Noah, while the ark was being prepared, in which a few, that is, eight souls, were saved through water. There is also an antitype which now saves us — baptism (not the removal of the filth of the flesh, but the answer of a good conscience toward God), through the resurrection of Jesus Christ, who has gone into heaven and is at the right hand of God, angels and authorities and powers having been made subject to Him
>
> (1 Peter 3:20-22, NKJV).

So, then, we see that the waters of the Flood point forward to the New Testament sacrament of baptism.

What we see, then, is the following pattern unfolding in the Scriptures. At the creation, water and Spirit appear together — the Spirit of God hovered over the face of the deep. At the Flood, water cleansed the creation and the presence of the Spirit and Noah released a dove, a symbol for the Holy Spirit. Peter also connects the Flood with the waters of baptism. This biblical imagery is packaged together in the placement and use of the bronze basin, which was to be used by the priests for the symbolic cleansing from sin.

Now, what we do not see all that clearly in the bronze basin is the idea of the presence of the Holy Spirit. But where we see the idea of water, or baptism, connected with the work of the Holy Spirit is later in the Old Testament prophets. Recall what God said through the prophet Ezekiel about how he would cleanse Israel from her sins. God told his people through Ezekiel that he would sprinkle clean water upon them and cleanse them from their sins, from their idolatries. But Ezekiel also told the people that this cleansing of water imagery was connected to the giving of the Holy Spirit, as God would give to them a new spirit within them; he would remove their heart of stone and give to them a heart of flesh (Ezek. 36:25-28).

When we put all of this biblical data together, there are clear correlations between the employment of water and the work of the Holy Spirit. The water-Spirit connection is something that recurs throughout all of Scripture. It appears at the creation, the Flood, the Red Sea crossing and, especially, the baptism of Christ. When we meditate upon the bronze laver in this broader scriptural context, the connections to baptism and the work of the Spirit make more sense. Additionally, when we read the prophet Ezekiel speak of cleansing the people of God in terms of sprinkling them with water and placing the Holy Spirit within them, the water-Spirit statements make sense against this broader backdrop of the rest of Scripture.

The bronze basin in the light of the New Testament

Water and Spirit in the New Testament

I think we can now appreciate some of the New Testament's statements regarding baptism. From what we see foreshadowed in the Old Testament, particularly in the bronze laver and its connections to the waters of creation and work of the Holy Spirit, a theology of baptism emerges very clearly in the light of the revelation of Jesus Christ.

Think of the connection between water and Spirit in the baptism of Christ. John the Baptist told the crowds that he baptized with water but that Christ would baptize with the Holy Spirit (Mark 1:8). Reflect upon Christ's instruction to Nicodemus when he told him that a person had to be born of both water and the Spirit in order to enter the kingdom of God (John 3:3-5). Paul uses language quite similar to that of John and Jesus, and even evocative of the washings performed at the bronze basin in the Old Testament tabernacle when he writes to Titus that we are saved, not because of works, but according to the mercy of God, 'by the washing of regeneration and renewal of the Holy Spirit, whom he poured out on us richly through Jesus Christ our Saviour' (Titus 3:4-7).

The New Testament has other such references that place water and the work of the Holy Spirit together. Jesus told the crowds at the feast of booths during the water-drawing ceremony, a remembrance of God's provision of water during Israel's time on the exodus in the arid and parched wilderness, that anyone who came to him for drink would never thirst but would have streams of living water flow from their heart. Especially instructive is John's interpretive comment: 'Now this he said about the Spirit, whom those who believed in him were to receive, for as yet the Spirit had not been given, because Jesus was not yet glorified' (John 7:39).

Putting it all together

Throughout all of Scripture there are clear links between the work of the Holy Spirit and water. Here with the bronze laver, therefore, we have a shadowy image of the work of the Holy Spirit, applying the redemptive work of Christ. Recall that the priests would not only offer a sacrifice, but they would also wash their hands and feet — signalling their ceremonial and ritual cleansing of sin.

Baptism points to the work of Christ and the Holy Spirit, which cleanses us from sin and sanctifies us — makes us holy. To be sure, the water of baptism neither removes sin nor saves us. Rather, the water of the bronze laver pointed to the work of Christ and the Holy Spirit. So too the water of baptism does not save but instead points to the saving work of Christ as it is applied by the work of the Holy Spirit. These redemptive realities, the work of Christ, the Holy Spirit, the cleansing from sin, and being set apart or sanctified prominently appear together when Paul writes to the church in Rome:

> *What shall we say then? Are we to continue in sin that grace may abound? By no means! How can we who died to sin still live in it? Do you not know that all of us who have been baptized into Christ Jesus were baptized into his death? We were buried therefore with him by baptism into death, in order that, just as Christ was raised from the dead by the glory of the Father, we too might walk in newness of life.*

For if we have been united with him in a death like his, we shall certainly be united with him in a resurrection like his. We know that our old self was crucified with him in order that the body of sin might be brought to nothing, so that we would no longer be enslaved to sin. For one who has died has been set free from sin. Now if we have died with Christ, we believe that we will also live with him. We know that Christ being raised from the dead will never die again; death no longer has dominion over him

(Rom. 6:1-9).

So, then, when we look at the bronze basin, and the water the priests used ceremonially to cleanse themselves from sin, our minds should ultimately fall upon the redemptive work of Christ and its application by the Holy Spirit, all of which is connected to our baptism.

As we reflect upon baptism, we should be drawn to the saving work of Christ through the Spirit. But in addition to reflecting upon the work of Christ and the Spirit, we should ask how we might be further sanctified, what older theologians called 'improving our baptism'. The authors of the *Westminster Larger Catechism*, written in the seventeenth century, ask the following question: 'How is our baptism to be improved by us?' They give the following answer:

The needful but much neglected duty of improving our baptism, is to be performed by us all our life long, especially in the time of temptation, and when we are present at the administration of it to others; by serious and thankful consideration of the nature of it, and of the ends for which Christ instituted it, the privileges and benefits conferred and sealed thereby, and our solemn vow made therein; by being humbled for our sinful defilement, our falling short of, and walking contrary

> *to, the grace of baptism, and our engagements; by growing up to assurance of pardon of sin, and of all other blessings sealed to us in that sacrament; by drawing strength from the death and resurrection of Christ, into whom we are baptized, for the mortifying of sin, and quickening of grace; and by endeavouring to live by faith, to have our conversation in holiness and righteousness, as those that have therein given up their names to Christ; and to walk in brotherly love, as being baptized by the same Spirit into one body*
>
> (q. 167).

In sole reliance upon the grace of God in Christ, through word, sacraments and prayer, we should therefore strive to improve upon our baptism.

For example, so many people in the church think of baptism in an individualistic sense. In other words, when a person is baptized, many believe the only person to benefit is the one who gets wet. The rest of the congregation are merely spectators sitting idly by as they wait for the worship service to resume. But if question 167 of the *Larger Catechism* is at all instructive, then when we are present at the baptism of others, we should meditate upon what it means, reflect upon our own baptism, but especially reflect upon the work of Christ and the Holy Spirit.

We should recall our own sinfulness and need for the washing regeneration of the Holy Spirit. When we see our covenant children baptized, we should pray that God would bring his covenant promises to pass, plant faith in the heart of the child, and wash the child with the regenerating and sanctifying work of the Holy Spirit. We should also reflect upon the life, death and resurrection of Christ and acknowledge that as Christ has been crucified, so we have been crucified, which means we have died to sin. Likewise, we have also been raised with Christ by the power of the Holy Spirit, which means that we have been raised to walk in the newness of life.

For these reasons the *Larger Catechism* states: 'The mortifying of sin, and quickening of grace; and by endeavouring to live by faith, to have our conversation in holiness and righteousness, as those that have therein given up their names to Christ; and to walk in brotherly love, as being baptized by the same Spirit into one body.' In other words, just as the washing at the bronze basin reminded the priests of their need for holiness, likewise we should come to the same conclusions. However, we should rejoice knowing that the outpouring of the Holy Spirit undergirds our own sanctification in a far greater way, both qualitatively and quantitatively, in comparison to the saints of the Old Testament.

Conclusion

When an Old Testament priest entered the confines of the tabernacle, he entered not only by the shedding of blood but also by the washing of water. Well, for anyone who enters the church, he enters by the shed blood of Jesus Christ and its application by the Holy Spirit, which is visually represented in the sacrament of baptism. In the same way a priest would meditate upon his need for sacrifice and washing, let us meditate upon our need for Christ and the Holy Spirit when we see a baptism performed. And, let us strive, as our fathers in the faith have instructed, to improve upon our baptism.

12

OHOLIAB AND BEZALEL

Read Exodus 31:1-11

Introduction

Over the last several chapters we have explored the various aspects of the instructions for the construction of the tabernacle and its practices. With each element of the tabernacle God typically gave Moses dimensions and even blueprints, if you will, for the tabernacle. We know this from what we read in the Exodus narrative: 'And see that you make them after the pattern for them, which is being shown you on the mountain' (Exod. 25:40). What we have in the passage before us is the equipping of the artisans to make the tabernacle with all of its furnishings. In other words, God not only gave Moses and the Israelites the plans for the tabernacle but also the ability to construct it.

The ability to construct the tabernacle, however, required no ordinary gifts. Rather, the ability came from the divine inspiration of the Holy Spirit. In exploring this aspect of the construction of the tabernacle, we will see the important connections to the person and work of Christ, and of course, us, the church. We will see that just as God gifted Oholiab and Bezalel with the inspiration of the Holy Spirit, so too he continues to provide the people of God with like-gifted individuals within the body of Christ, the church. God gives his people spiritual gifts so that they can build the final dwelling place of God, the final temple, the church. Let us explore the narrative and see these connections to Christ, the Holy Spirit, and the church.

The tabernacle artisans

When we look at the narrative we see that God called Bezalel, which means 'in God's shadow', and Oholiab, which means, 'the father is my tent', which seem to be apt names for those who would work on the tabernacle. What is of particular interest, however, is that God tells Moses: 'I have filled him with the Spirit of God, with ability and intelligence, with knowledge and all craftsmanship' (Exod. 31:3). God's statement is of significance because it indicates that he filled the two men 'with the Spirit of God'. Now, to us, this may not seem all that significant because we are accustomed to reading about the person and work of the Holy Spirit. The phrase, however, is not all that common in the Old Testament, occurring only about a dozen times; although, it most prominently occurs with the creation of the heavens and earth in Genesis 1:1ff. There are, then, some interesting parallels between the creation of the heavens and earth, which involved the superintendence of the Holy Spirit, and the creation of the tabernacle, which was a microcosmic reproduction of the creation, also involving the work of the Holy Spirit.

What, however, did the Holy Spirit specifically inspire Oholiab and Bezalel to do? Well, we see from verses 2 onwards that he gave them ability, intelligence, knowledge and all craftsmanship to make designs, work in gold, silver, and bronze, cut stones, and carve wood. So, these two men were specifically gifted by inspiration of the Holy Spirit to carry out the construction of the tabernacle. We also read in verse 6 that God gave other men the ability to carry out what he had commanded them to do. Now, let us consider this event in the light of the revelation of Christ.

The temple artisans in the light of the New Testament

I have heard this passage interpreted by another theologian who made the connection between the inspiration of the Holy Spirit and the arts. In other words, God is a God of beauty and we see his great interest in the arts; after all, one of the first references to the inspiration of the Holy Spirit is connected to artistic abilities. There are at least two problems with this interpretation.

First, it does not explain how unbelievers, who quite obviously also have great artistic abilities, receive their talent. It is one thing to say that God gives his creatures many talents and abilities but it is quite another to say that unbelievers are inspired by the Holy Spirit and given artistic abilities. It creates a real theological mess when one finds an artist who is talented, but then uses those supposedly Holy Spirit-inspired talents for something other than the glory of God.

Second, such an interpretation fails to consider the broader scriptural context of this narrative. Whenever we look at the Old Testament tabernacle and temple, we must remember we are looking at a shadowy image, or type, of Christ and the church. We see this interpretive trajectory most clearly when Paul writes: 'So then you are no longer strangers and aliens, but you are fellow citizens with the saints and members of the household of God, built on the foundation of the apostles and prophets, Christ Jesus himself being the cornerstone, in whom the whole structure, being joined together, grows into a holy temple in the Lord. In him you also are being built together into a dwelling place for God by the Spirit' (Eph. 2:19-22). So, then, taking this interpretive clue, we can reorient the inspiration of the Holy Spirit in the following manner.

The Holy Spirit gave Oholiab and Bezalel the gifts they needed to construct the tabernacle. Well, the Holy Spirit continues this same activity, though in a slightly different way. Paul tells the Corinthians: 'Now there are varieties of gifts, but the same Spirit; and there are varieties of service, but the same Lord; and there are varieties of activities, but it is the same God who empowers them all in everyone. To each is given the manifestation of the Spirit for the common good' (1 Cor. 12:4-7). Notice that Paul explains that the Holy Spirit dispenses gifts, but that the gifts of the Spirit are 'for the common good'. Paul exhorts the Corinthians to use their gifts to build up the church: 'So with yourselves, since you are eager for manifestations of the Spirit, strive to excel in building up the church' (1 Cor. 14:12). In terms of the Old Testament shadow, Oholiab and Bezalel were to use their gifts of the Spirit to build the tabernacle. In the light of the revelation of Christ, Oholiab and Bezalel foreshadow the spiritual endowment of the people of God to build the church, the final temple and dwelling place of God. Now what types of gifts of the Spirit do we see Paul identify?

Before we identify the gifts of the Spirit, it is important that we distinguish the gifts of the Spirit from the fruit of the Spirit. The fruit of the Spirit is: love, joy, peace, patience, kindness, goodness, faithfulness, gentleness and self-control (Gal. 5:22-23). All believers, young, old, man, woman, adult, child, are supposed to manifest the fruit of the Spirit. The gifts of the Spirit, on the other hand, are the unique gifts and abilities that the Holy Spirit gives to people in the church for its edification. In 1 Corinthians 12 Paul identifies several of these gifts:

Utterances of wisdom (v. 8a) — likely the ability to resolve difficult spiritual problems;
Utterances of knowledge (v. 8b) — the comprehension of doctrinal matters;
Faith (v. 9a) — not faith in general, as it is a fruit of the Spirit, but a

greater dispensation of faith in the face of profound trial — the faith of a mustard seed — one that can move mountains;

Healing (v. 9b) — the ability to heal others of disease or sickness;

Working of miracles (v. 10a) — the ability, for example, to raise someone from death;

Prophecy (v. 10b) — giving utterance to special revelation — words that would be of the same authority with Scripture itself;

Discernment (v. 10c) — the ability to discern spiritual good from evil;

Various kinds of tongues (v. 10d) — the ability to speak in a known language without ever having studied it;

Interpretation of tongues (v. 10e) — the ability to interpret a known language without ever having studied it.

These gifts were not universally dispensed but were sovereignly given by the Holy Spirit to the individuals whom he chose. And, as Paul said, these gifts were not for personal pride, or personal advancement or goals, but for the mutual edification of the church.

This list from 1 Corinthians 12 that Paul gives, however, is not exhaustive. Paul gives a second list of the gifts of the Spirit in Romans: 'Having gifts that differ according to the grace given to us, let us use them: if prophecy, in proportion to our faith; if service, in our serving; the one who teaches, in his teaching; the one who exhorts, in his exhortation; the one who contributes, in generosity; the one who leads, with zeal; the one who does acts of mercy, with cheerfulness' (Rom. 12:6-8). Notice there is a repetition of some of the same gifts Paul listed in 1 Corinthians 12, but there are also other gifts:

Service (v. 7a) — the specific Greek word behind the English is the one we find used for where we get the word, *deacon*, which means serving, both generally and specifically (i.e., the diaconate);

Teaching (v. 7b) — teaching others the Word of God, whether women teaching children, fathers teaching their families, or elders teaching the church;

Exhorting (v. 8a) — is a gift where one encourages others to obedience to the revealed will of God;

Contributing (v. 8b) — giving financially to the church;

Leading (v. 8c) — which specifically refers to the ability to lead others, which can be given to both men and women, though it is only men who exercise this gift over the church;

Acts of mercy (v. 8d) — showing mercy to others can take on a number of forms.

There is still a third list of spiritual gifts: 'And he gave the apostles, the prophets, the evangelists, the pastors and teachers, to equip the saints for the work of ministry, for building up the body of Christ' (Eph. 4:11-12). Notice that Paul says that the apostles, New Testament prophets, evangelists, pastors and teachers have all been given to equip the saints for the work of ministry and to build the body of Christ. In other words, the gifts of the Spirit are not simply abilities but also offices, pastors and teachers.

So, then, given this trajectory throughout the Scriptures, God has continued to give the gifts of the Holy Spirit to his people for the construction of his dwelling place, whether the Old Testament tabernacle in the Sinai desert, or the final temple, the church, the body of Christ. As you can well imagine, this touches upon us, the church, in a powerful and direct way. The question that we should ask ourselves is: 'How will I use my spiritual gifts?' Will I use them for the building up of the temple of God, the church, or will I use them for my own benefit, pride and ego? The answer is quite clearly the former — we must use our spiritual gifts for constructing the church.

That means when we come to church, we do not come merely to be spectators or to be served. Rather, we come to church to serve, to build up the church. From the list of spiritual gifts, we can easily see that there are a myriad of ways that we might contribute, as there are a number of different spiritual gifts. We might be called to serve as an officer of the church — as an elder or deacon. We might exercise the gift of teaching — the children's Sunday school is an important place in a church. It is the place where future generations of God's people are being raised and taught the fear and admonition of the Lord. We might see a need in the church and act upon it — something as mundane as setting up tables and chairs for a worship service or fellowship meal. We might see someone in need, and in an act of mercy, pour out the love of the Holy Spirit upon others within the church. We might see a financial need and give not out of our abundance but sacrificially — such activity is a gift of the Spirit.

We should rejoice because just as God equipped Oholiab and Bezalel so they could build the tabernacle — that is, follow the commands that God gave them — so too he equips us with his Holy Spirit so we can carry out the work of building the church. There are two important things that we should never forget, though, when it comes to our use of the gifts of the Spirit. First, we must remember that there is no one in the body of Christ that is dispensable. If I may use medical language to make an analogy, there is no such thing as an appendix in the body of Christ. Paul is quite clear on this point:

> *All these are empowered by one and the same Spirit, who apportions to each one individually as he wills. For just as the body is one and has many members, and all the members of the body, though many, are one body, so it is with Christ. For in one Spirit we were all baptized into one body — Jews or Greeks, slaves or free — and all were made to drink of one Spirit.*

> *For the body does not consist of one member but of many. If the foot should say, 'Because I am not a hand, I do not belong to the body', that would not make it any less a part of the body. And if the ear should say, 'Because I am not an eye, I do not belong to the body', that would not make it any less a part of the body. If the whole body were an eye, where would be the sense of hearing? If the whole body were an ear, where would be the sense of smell? But as it is, God arranged the members in the body, each one of them, as he chose. If all were a single member, where would the body be? As it is, there are many parts, yet one body*
>
> (1 Cor. 12:11-20).

Second, not only must we use the gifts of the Spirit for the mutual edification of the body of Christ, but we must do so in love. Without love, the use of our spiritual gifts is a waste of time and energy:

> *And God has appointed in the church first apostles, second prophets, third teachers, then miracles, then gifts of healing, helping, administrating, and various kinds of tongues. Are all apostles? Are all prophets? Are all teachers? Do all work miracles? Do all possess gifts of healing? Do all speak with tongues? Do all interpret? But earnestly desire the higher gifts.*
>
> *And I will show you a still more excellent way.*
>
> *If I speak in the tongues of men and of angels, but have not love, I am a noisy gong or a clanging cymbal. And if I have prophetic powers, and understand all mysteries and all knowledge, and if I have all faith, so as to remove mountains, but have not love, I am nothing. If I give away all I have, and if I deliver up my body to be burned, but have not love, I gain nothing.*

Love is patient and kind; love does not envy or boast; it is not arrogant or rude. It does not insist on its own way; it is not irritable or resentful; it does not rejoice at wrongdoing, but rejoices with the truth. Love bears all things, believes all things, hopes all things, endures all things.

Love never ends

(1 Cor. 12:28 - 13:8).

Conclusion

As we read the narrative of the endowment of Oholiab and Bezalel, our minds should eventually fall upon the final dwelling place of God, the church, founded upon the apostles and prophets, with Christ as the cornerstone. We should rejoice that God has given us the gifts of the Holy Spirit to carry out the construction of the church. We should therefore come to church with the desire to serve and to build up the body of Christ. We should remember to use our gifts in humility, as we all need one another. And, we should exercise our gifts in love to the glory of our triune Lord.

13

THE SABBATH

Read Exodus 31:12-18

Introduction

We at last come to the conclusion of the tabernacle instruction narratives. We have seen the instructions for the tabernacle, its furnishings and rituals. We have explored how each aspect of the tabernacle in some way points to the person and work of Christ, its application by the Holy Spirit and, of course, the church. Jesus Christ is the chief cornerstone of the last and final temple, the church, which is built upon the foundation of the apostles and prophets, and is being constructed with us, living stones, into a spiritual house. What may seem peculiar, however, is that the tabernacle instruction narratives end with further instructions about the Sabbath. It seems peculiar because God revealed the Sabbath command, the fourth command, in the Ten Commandments.

Why, if God gave Israel the fourth commandment in the law, do the tabernacle instruction narratives end with directions regarding the Sabbath? The simple answer is that God reveals *more* information about the Sabbath. Let us look at the added elements and also consider why God once again places emphasis on the Sabbath.

And, as we have with all of the other elements of the tabernacle, we will explore the connections to Christ and to us, the church.

The significance of the Sabbath

A sign of sanctification

The narrative begins with God reminding Moses about the importance of the Sabbath: 'You are to speak to the people of Israel and say, "Above all you shall keep my Sabbaths, for this is a sign between me and you throughout your generations, that you may know that I, the Lord, sanctify you"' (Exod. 31:13). When God reminds the Israelites about the Sabbath, we read about information they have not received before. When we read the fourth commandment, for example, we see that there is no mention of the Sabbath serving as a sign:

> 'Remember the Sabbath day, to keep it holy. Six days you shall labour, and do all your work, but the seventh day is a Sabbath to the Lord your God. On it you shall not do any work, you, or your son, or your daughter, your male servant, or your female servant, or your livestock, or the sojourner who is within your gates. For in six days the Lord made heaven and earth, the sea, and all that is in them, and rested the seventh day. Therefore the Lord blessed the Sabbath day and made it holy'
> (Exod. 20:8-11).

We simply see the prohibition of work and the reminder that the Israelites were supposed to remember that God worked six days and rested on the Sabbath. Notice, though, that God here tells Moses that the Sabbath is a sign.

What is a sign? Well, it is some sort of visual symbol of God's promises among his people: the tree of life, for example, was a visual sign of God's covenant promise of life to Adam. The rainbow was a visual sign of God's covenant promise to Noah and the creation not to destroy the earth by a flood again. Circumcision was a visual sign of God's covenant promise to Abraham. Here God identifies the Sabbath as a visual sign. A sign of what? A visual sign that God was sanctifying Israel — setting them apart and making them holy. In other words, God had redeemed Israel from Egypt, was placing himself in their midst, and had given them an avenue of approach through the tabernacle.

When I write of an avenue of approach, I mean that God had provided a means of atonement for them. In other words, Israel was not redeemed so that they could be like the other pagan nations; Israel was to be a 'kingdom of priests and a holy nation' (Exod. 19:6). They were to be holy as God was holy. How, though, was the Sabbath to serve as a sign that God was sanctifying Israel? If God's previous signs of the covenant were clearly visible — a tree, rainbow and circumcision — in what way can a period of time be visible?

The idea was that Israel would cease from its daily labours and rest. Israel's cessation from her labour was the visual sign — the sign that showed the nations around her that God was sanctifying Israel. Now, the cessation from labour was not merely a suggestion but a command, as anyone who laboured on the Sabbath was to be put to death: 'You shall keep the Sabbath, because it is holy for you. Everyone who profanes it shall be put to death. Whoever does any work on it, that soul shall be cut off from among his people' (Exod. 31:14). Not only was the violator put to death, but he was also cut off from the covenant community as well. Just as with circumcision, the infant male who was not circumcised on the eighth day was cut off from the covenant, so too the one who disrespected the sign of the Mosaic covenant, the Sabbath, was cut off from the covenant. This may seem harsh, but when we think about the Sabbath as a sign that God was sanctifying Israel, it makes more sense.

The Israelites were not supposed to work because they were not able to enter God's eternal rest by their own labour, but only by the labour of another. This is something that we will explore in greater detail below. The Sabbath as a sign of the covenant was not a temporary institution but Israel was to keep the Sabbath 'throughout their generations, as a covenant for ever' (v. 16). The Sabbath, then, served as a sign that God was sanctifying Israel, but this was not the only thing to which the Sabbath pointed.

A sign of the end

God tells Moses that the Sabbath was also supposed to be a sign that pointed back to the original rest of God: 'It is a sign for ever between me and the people of Israel that in six days the LORD made heaven and earth, and on the seventh day he rested and was refreshed' (Exod. 31:17). The Sabbath was supposed to be a sign of God's eternal rest, the rest he entered on the seventh day of the initial creation week. Notice the double-emphasis upon God's rest — 'he rested and was refreshed'. That God calls the Sabbath a sign of his rest is an important reminder. It does not simply remind us that God worked six days and then rested — in other words, a reminder that God was creator — it was more specifically a reminder that God had a goal for the creation.

Before sin ever entered the world, God had an end in mind. Adam was supposed to do the work that God commanded, complete his work, and then rest as God did. Adam, however, never completed the work. God was telling Israel that he, not man, would bring Israel into his eternal rest. The overall intended message of the Sabbath as a sign was that God was at work in the midst of Israel, sanctifying his people, bringing them to the completion of their journey — his own heavenly rest.

The Sabbath in the light of the New Testament

God, the second person of the Trinity, has accomplished the work that Adam failed to do on behalf of the people of God. When Christ stood up in the synagogue and read the passage of Isaiah regarding the year of Jubilee and pronounced that the passage had been fulfilled in their midst, he was announcing that he was the one who was doing the work. Christ was announcing that he was bringing the long-awaited redemption and final rest for the people of God. This is why Christ told those who followed him: 'Come to me, all who labour and are heavy laden, and I will give you rest' (Matt. 11:28). This is why the author of Hebrews tells his readers: 'For we who have believed enter that rest' (Heb. 4:3). In other words, when we place our faith in Christ, we begin to enter the Sabbath rest of God, but we do so, not by our own labours, but by the labour of another — Jesus Christ.

Yet, we also know that even though we begin to enter the rest of God, there is still a sense in which we have not completely entered his eternal rest: 'So then, there remains a Sabbath rest for the people of God' (Heb. 4:9). Our relation to the Sabbath rest of God is much like our salvation — there is a sense in which we are saved, we are being saved, and we will be saved. Or I can put it like this: we are justified, are being sanctified, and will be glorified. It is this type of relationship that we have with the Sabbath — we have entered it, which is why the author to the Hebrews says that we who have believed enter his rest. There is still yet a Sabbath rest for the people of God, which means that there will come a time when we have completely entered God's rest. Now, keeping these things in mind, let us contemplate the instructions that Moses receives regarding the Sabbath in the light of Christ.

CHRIST AND THE DESERT TABERNACLE

A sign of sanctification

We, as the people of God, no longer observe the Sabbath, or day of rest, on the last day of the week. Because Christ has come and completed the work on our behalf by fulfilling every jot and tittle of the law, paid the penalty for sin, been raised from the dead, and has ascended to the right hand of the Father, we now observe our day of rest on the first day of the week. What is important to see is that the day of rest, what we now call 'the Lord's Day', or Sunday, is still a sign that God is sanctifying us. Each Lord's Day we rest from our labours and look specifically to the one who has done the work on our behalf, Jesus Christ. But by coming to church and gathering for worship, we should both tacitly and explicitly admit that God is in our presence sanctifying us. God sanctifies us in a number of ways.

God sanctifies us, or sets us apart, because no other gathering of people, except for the gathering of the church, is the place where we find God's special holy presence. When we absent ourselves from church and fail to observe the Lord's Day, we are tacitly admitting that we have no desire to be in the presence of God. God sanctifies us by the power, presence and work of his Holy Spirit. We are not simply saved from sin and death and then left to ourselves to work out our salvation. On the contrary, God is the one who conforms us to the image of his Son by the work of the Holy Spirit.

Each and every Lord's Day that we gather together is a visible sign that God is at work in our midst — that he is conforming us to the image of his Son. We remind ourselves and the tell the world around us that we need our triune Lord to feed us, to speak to us, to forgive us of our sin, to comfort us with his presence, and to sanctify us — to make us more like Christ. When we absent ourselves from church and fail to observe the Lord's Day, we are tacitly admitting that we do not need the sanctifying work of God in our lives. We must realize that we *do* need that sanctifying work of our triune Lord. In the same way that we show respect for the covenant sign of baptism and for the sacrament of the Lord's Supper, should we not show the same care and attentiveness to the Lord's Day, a sign of God's sanctifying work on our behalf?

A sign of the end

We should also realize that the Lord's Day is, like it was for Israel, a sign of the end; in other words, that we do not go about our lives as with the pagan religions — never knowing any rest. Many pagan religions never have an end, such as the idea of reincarnation. A person never knows rest but simply is reincarnated over and over and over again. Yet the Lord's Day is a sign of the end — the rest of God into which we will one day finally and completely enter.

We need to think of it in the following terms. God gave Moses the instructions for the observance of the Sabbath at the conclusion of the instructions for the tabernacle. This organization is significant — remember that the tabernacle foreshadows the person of work and the church. The implied message is that the temple that my Son will build, the church, will have an ending point. This means that the Lord's Day, Sunday, still serves the same purpose. Each and every Lord's Day, we stop from our labours, we look back upon the finished work of Christ, worship our triune Lord in celebration of that work, but we also look forward to the second coming of Christ, to the end of all things. We look forward anticipating the end — our final and total entrance into the rest of God. How often do we long for heaven itself but pass by the Lord's Day as an opportunity to get a taste of heaven — to rest from our labours, to hear the Lord speak to us, to fellowship with God's people, and worship our triune Lord? These are all things that we will be doing in eternity. We must realize, then, that the fourth commandment is still binding upon the church and that it is still a sign of the covenant — a sign that God is sanctifying us and a sign that there is an end.

Death penalty and the Sabbath

We should take note, though, of one last item, namely, the death penalty and the Sabbath. We sometimes look at the death penalty for Sabbath-breaking and think God was too harsh. But remember, the relationship of the Old Testament to the New Testament is one of shadow and reality. The shadow for breaking the Sabbath in the Old Testament was death. The reality for breaking the Lord's Day in the New Testament is eternal death. In other words, the one who tries to enter the Lord's rest, the eternal Sabbath, by his own work rather than the work of Christ will merit only condemnation. For the wages of sin is death, but the free gift of God in Christ Jesus is eternal life.

Conclusion

My prayer is that we will have a full-orbed understanding of the Sabbath — that we would understand why we cease from our labours. We cease from our labours because we are recognizing that the Lord's Day is a sign that our triune Lord is sanctifying us and that there is an end. It is a sign that Christ has come and done the work on behalf of the people of God and that he will return and bring an end to all things. Though we have entered the rest of God by faith in Christ, let us heed the exhortation of the author of Hebrews: 'So then, there remains a Sabbath rest for the people of God, for whoever has entered God's rest has also rested from his works as God did from his. Let us therefore strive to enter that rest, so that no one may fall by the same sort of disobedience' (Heb. 4:9-11). Let us look to Christ in faith — the one who has completed the work. Let us observe the Lord's Day with great joy, knowing that it is a visible sign to the world around us that God is sanctifying us. Let us observe the Lord's Day with great excitement, knowing that we are getting a taste of the end and that Christ will return to bring all things to an end.

CONCLUSION

The next time you read through the tabernacle narratives I hope you do so with great interest and excitement. Read these narratives in the knowledge that you are not reading boring plans and instructions about an irrelevant structure that no longer exists, but that you are reading about instructions and shadowy pictures of the person and work of Christ. You are also reading about the church, the final temple and dwelling place of God that has Christ as the chief cornerstone with the apostles and prophets as the foundation, a temple being built together into a dwelling place for the triune Lord. In other words, always read the Old Testament in the light of the New Testament. St Augustine, one of the early Church Fathers, once wrote that what is hidden in the Old is revealed in the New, and what is revealed in the New is hidden in the Old. If you read these tabernacle narratives in the light of the New Testament you will see them in the light of Christ. SDG.

Also from the author…

The fruit of the Spirit is...

Every Christian should desire to manifest godliness and the fruit of the Spirit. Yet too often we try to achieve it by mere good intentions, and efforts to pull ourselves up by our moral bootstraps. Such attempts always fall short of spiritual reality.

Godliness should be a defining characteristic of Christians, so how does one obtain it?

In this fascinating work John Fesko shows us that godliness comes through the work of the Holy Spirit and manifests itself as the fruit of the Spirit. We do not produce this fruit on our own, but rather Christ through his Spirit produces it in us.

As he looks at Paul's famous fruit of the Spirit passage in Galatians 5, the author shows that this work of the Spirit is not merely a New Testament idea, but is written throughout the pages of Old Testament history, from creation, the Exodus, through the prophets, to the fulfilment of promised blessings in the work of the Lord Jesus. When this fruit is displayed in our lives, we are experiencing and manifesting the very things God promised over 2,500 years ago.

The fruit of the Spirit is..., 80 pages, ISBN: 978-0-85234-736-2, EP Books.

A wide range of Christian books is available from EP Books. If you would like a free catalogue please write to us or contact us by e-mail. Alternatively, you can view the whole catalogue online at our web site.

www.epbooks.org

EP BOOKS
Faverdale North
Darlington, DL3 0PH, England

e-mail: sales@epbooks.org